Be Fire Safe

by Steven C. Shepard, Ph.D.

Ronin Publishing
Berkeley, CA.

Be Fire Safe!
ISBN: 1-57951-054-X
Copyright © 2002 by Steven C. Shepard

Published by
RONIN Publishing, Inc.
PO Box 522
Berkeley, CA 94701
roninpub.com

Credits:

Project Editor:	**Beverly A. Potter**	
	docpotter.com	
Cover Design:	**Judy July, Generic Type**	
	generictype.com	
Fonts:	Gouty	
	Helvetica	
	Quetzalcoati	

Distributed to the trade by **Publishers Group West**
Printed in the United States of America by **Bertelsmann**
Library of Congress Card Number: 2002090486

Table of Contents

DEDICATION

This book is dedicated to my mother, Lois, who saved our lives, and my wife, Patricia, and daughter, Tara, who's inspiration kept us moving forward.

 Never a Good Time

There is a terrible irony in the way the fire changed my life. Not only did it rage through our house when least expected, but it happened at the worst possible time—three days after the bank sent a warning notice: *"Your insurance has been cancelled"* and instructed us to send a new certificate of homeowner's insurance.

I lived with my wife, Patricia, my mother, Lois and our two cats, Herbie, and Misty in a beautiful 5-bedroom two-story stucco home on a tree-lined cul-de-sac. We were already overloaded with difficulties. I still had a cast on my arm from an auto accident that totaled my car just a month before. My mother was recovering from a recent stroke triggered by medication she had taken to treat breast cancer. It was not a good time for a fire.

Bureaucratic Limbo

We loved our beautiful home.

We loved our beautiful home we'd worked so hard for. The threat that our insurance may have expired terrified me. I had gotten a run around when I called the insurance company the day before because we didn't have an assigned agent. When no one returned my call, I called again to be told they didn't have my file. I asked if I could deliver a check but the agent said he had to investigate since the company was not issuing new coverage. "Don't worry," he said. "We'll get this straightened out." I resolved to take care of it the next morning. Little did I know that the next day would be too late.

In the Eye of a Firestorm

Shortly after 1 a.m., Patricia threw clothes in the dryer in the garage— as she had done hundreds of times—turned the lights off and came up to help me shower. My arm had been broken in the car accident a month earlier and was held in the air by a cast. Ordinary activities like showering and getting dressed were nearly impossible for me to do without help.

As Mother was falling asleep, she heard a booming sound. With considerable difficulty she got up to investigate. Smoke was coming through the wall. Grasping and stumbling with her walker, she rushed to the bathroom door and yelled: "Fire! Fire! Steve! Smoke and flames are coming through the wall!"

With no time to dry off, I grabbed a pair of jeans and Patricia threw a towel around herself as we rushed out to see the smoke—now billowing up the stairway. Moments later a smoke alarm triggered a loud wailing siren. Through a window, I saw the horror of our neighbor's house being lit up by the flashing orange flames dancing on *our* blazing home.

Just Get Out!

The realization was terrible. *Our house was on fire!* It was overwhelming. We had to run for our lives. "Get Out! Just get out!" I yelled to my wife and mother. I remembered our two cats and rushed into our bedroom to look for them. Misty, a Norwegian forest cat, was sitting wide-eyed on our bed. Giving a terrified yelp, she bolted down the hall. Yelling and running behind her, I snatched her up.

Suddenly, we were in total blackness. All the lights went out when the fire burned the electrical panel. Coughing from smoke, we stumbled down the stairs to the front door. Someone was banging on the door and yelling, "Get out! Get out!" It was Joe, from across the street.

We Were Trapped

We had a double deadbolt lock on the door that required a key to unlock it. It was locked! Paralyzed in the total darkness—in a near panic—we had to *find* the key. Where was it?

Patricia groped in the dark—feeling for the key. *Finally*, she found it but in the confusion, choking on smoke, she dropped it. Struggling to hold the towel around her naked body, Patricia felt around the floor in the dark feeling for the key. The fire was closing in on us as we choked and gasped for air.

After what seemed like a lifetime, Patricia found the key. Thank God! But she still had to unlock the deadbolt—easy to do under normal conditions—but in the dark with the fire looming, it felt like we were living a Stephen King episode.

After several attempts, Patricia succeeded unlocking the door. We pulled it open and stumbled out. Joe steadied my mother, then he grabbed Misty from me.

 Chaos

We were in a state of shock, trembling, and suffering from smoke inhalation. Patricia sat down, coughing, sick, and throwing up from the smoke and stress. Numb, I stood on the sidewalk across from our burning house, surrounded by neighbors offering to help. Immobilized by grief and loss, I could only stare ahead.

Where's Herbie?

"Where was our cat, Herbie?" I felt the panic rise up through me. I was terrified we'd lose him. A crowd of concerned neighbors yelled at me not to go back. Ignoring reason, I plunged back into our smoky, flaming house. Patricia, still wearing only a towel, rushed in behind me to get her clothes.

With my eyes burning, I spotted Herbie through the smoke cowering under Mother's hospital bed. But he was so terrified that he pulled back. Ignoring the cast on my arm, I tried to lift the bed, but it was way too heavy to lift it with one hand. Coughing from the smoke filling the room, I realized I had only seconds left to get out.

Reluctantly, I left Herbie and ran down the stairs and out the front door, just behind Patricia who was now wrapped in a blanket that she grabbed from the bed when she couldn't find her clothes in the smoke and darkness. At least *we* were safe.

Thinking back on it now that I am safe and clear thinking, it was a reckless decision to risk our lives for clothes and a cat. But we weren't thinking.

Fire Trucks Arrive

Police arrived and set up the command post to evacuate the neighborhood. Firemen rushed towards the house with their hoses to extinguish the blaze. More police cars sped up, sirens wailing, along with three ambulances. A local TV station cameraman appeared and began taping.

Watching Helplessly

Flames kept shooting up, especially from the garage. As firemen forced one column of flames into retreat, another one would erupt.

Firemen attacked the fire with fierce volleys of water, until it slowly died down, leaving balls of smoke behind. Then they moved to another blazing section.

Sometimes, the fire appeared to be out, only to have a renewed blaze surge up. I can still hear the noise—loud kabooms, and blackened beams from the roof or the walls crashing down into the flames that gulped them up. Black soot swirled up and flew over the street. One by one the gas tanks on my cars exploded, adding more fuel to the fire. All we could do was to watch our dream house turn into a collapsing, blackened ruin. For many agonizing minutes, we were paralyzed in fear that the barbecue propane tanks would explode and ignite our neighbor's homes.

Supportive Neighbors

The outpouring of help from our neighbors made a tremendous difference in helping Patricia and me get through those darkest hours and keeping us going in the difficult days that followed. Having supporters is key to getting through a disaster situation. It is smart to build relationships with people you can count on, so that if a fire occurs, they are there for you.

An hour after the first 911 call most of the fire was contained. Part of the house was still standing. The garage where the fire started was a charred ruin and the once proud cars it housed were melted hulks. Half the roof had collapsed and what remained was too badly burned to salvage. The kitchen and bedroom above the garage were blacked and beyond repair, as was the attic. Nonetheless, much of the house still stood. It was too hot, smoky, and dark to enter. Firemen searched for signs of fire.

A Miracle

Miraculously, a fireman came out of the chard ruins holding a scared and bedraggled Herbie, who had managed to survive. Perhaps the hospital bed had protected him from the smoke and flames. Suddenly I remembered Misty and began worrying about her. Joe who had taken her from me when I ran out the front door. He said "She was so scared, she clawed her way out of my arms and ran down the street."

 Aftermath

A few fire engines and police cars remained. Reporters came and went through out the day with at least one crew filming most of the time.

A parade of reporters stopped me over the next several hours. Each had questions about our hair-raising escape. I welcomed their interest, thinking: "Maybe our story will help others facing a fire." Helping others to prevent the tragedy we experienced helped me feel that what had happened to us had not been in vain. By noon I had done about 30 interviews.

Insurance Steps In

Several reps from our insurance company arrived. There was an operations director to coordinate work on the site, an adjuster to inventory the salvageable contents, and a property claims rep to secure bids from contractors. With them was a laborer, whose job it was to dig through the rubble to locate items to be removed for restoration. The supervisor in charge of the case and the office paperwork handed me a check for $2500 to cover living expenses for the first few days. "I'll have more for you in a few days," she assured me.

The supervisor reassured me, "We'll take care of everything. We'll arrange for storage. Arrange for restorers to salvage what furniture and artwork as best they can. Just leave it to us, and we'll hire the contractors and pay them directly." I thought the insurance team was on the job. I was especially impressed that they exuded such confidence and knew what they were doing.

Looking at our smoldering home was wrenching. I saw the devastation and felt the dampness and smelled the musty odor of wet soot, burned lumber, melted plastic and smoldering furniture. The day before everything had been bright and cheerful—and still smelled good. The insurance officials went around with their clipboards making notes, like accountants doing an inventory; I was overwhelmed by the stark realization of the loss. At that moment my life seemed to be covered in sooty water.

Substantiating Our Loss

As we continued our walk-through I was struck by how much was irreplaceable. The realization of how difficult it was going to be

to substantiate our loss began to filter into my awareness. We didn't
have photographs or documents. The records had burned in the fire.
We never thought to keep our records at a separate location. Now
only memories remained of so many treasures. Later I would learn
how important documents are for proving damage and loss.

Securing the House

After their preliminary inspection, the insurance reps called in a
crew who spread huge sheets of plastic over the entire house. Other
workers nailed plywood over the outer walls, windows, and doors to
secure the house from theft. Yet more contractors appeared throughout the afternoon and evening to remove the collectibles and
artwork that were to be restored.

The insurance adjuster explained that the restorers would put
the reparable clothing and furniture in an ozone chamber to get out
the smell. The artwork would go to professional art restorers. The
insurance arranged for a replacement car to arrive later that afternoon.

🔥 Recovery

After the drama and intense aftermath of the fire,
the week that followed was one of healing and recovery.
We assessed where we were, determined what we had left,
and decided where to go from here. Our neighbors were wonderful.
They provided day-to-day help in assisting us, and the emotional
support of people who cared. I don't know how we would have
gotten through the crisis without them.

Clean Up

A clean-up crew carried furniture, artwork, and other items that
the adjuster identified as "totaled," along with fallen beams and
ashes to a large construction dumpster. It was wrenching to see our
things being put into a dumpster. On the walk-through, the insurance adjuster explained that the company preferred to total items
rather than try to salvage them. Precious items that could have been
saved were thrown in the dumpster, along with burned boards, soot,
water, nails, and pieces of ceiling material.

Less damaged items were loaded into a long van to take
them to a warehouse to be cleaned, restored, and de-smoked

of lingering fire smells. Most of our clothing had been destroyed, so we were left with only a few wearable items. We lost our files and computers.

The insurance rep explained that the company would calculate the average rents in the area for a house like ours, called "getting comps". This comparison would establish the rental value for our house and the amount we would be given to pay for rent until our house was rebuilt.

Neighbors Affected

We were not the only ones going through a recovery process—neighbors were also deeply distressed. Carol, who lived next door, was particularly affected. She had trouble sleeping, lost her appetite, and stayed inside much of the day. The image of our house burning and the memory of seeing her own house catch fire was seared into her mind.

Louie's wife, who had narrowly escaped a house fire as a child, was deeply distressed. Seeing our house engulfed in flames brought back terrible memories. In fact, most of our neighbors reported experiencing some emotional turmoil.

Worst Fears Manifest

By the week's end, we were gradually healing. The memory of the horror and despair of the first days were receding as we started to feel more hopeful. Then a week after the fire our world turned upside down again when Patricia and I stopped at the site to ask about our living expenses check. The claims supervisor looked nervous. Sensing a problem, I stiffened. "What's wrong?" I asked. Hesitating, like a doctor considering how to give bad news to a patient, she proceeded, "There's a coverage problem," she said. "I had to tell everyones to stop operations immediately."

I looked at her in stunned shock, scarcely believing what she was saying as she announced, "We won't be able to pay for any further work." "What about the items that have been taken to the warehouse for clean-up and restoration?" I asked. "Some of them are still wet, and if they're not dried and cleaned up quickly, they'll be even further damaged. And what about the items still in the house—the clothes, the piano, my mother's adjustable hospital bed?"

The supervisor nodded, "I'm sorry. But we can't do anything or pay for anything more until we determine if you are covered or not." With that the three insurance reps, along with all of the contractors stopped working and left. Suddenly, everything went into a terrible silence.

The news hit me like a bombshell. We were supposed to simply wait. As they disappeared down the street, Patricia and I stood there feeling lost and alone, looking at our house that lay eerily silent.

We Made Mistakes

We made many mistakes that contributed to the fire starting and spreading. It was sheer luck that we escaped. Because of our mistakes our escape was more precarious and more difficult. Worse, we went back into our burning house after we got out safely, which could have been a fatal mistake.

Several of our mistakes are ones that most people make, whether homeowners or renters. It can be difficult to think about potential problems and disasters. Thinking about damage, loss, and dangers that can result in property destruction or loss of lives is not a pleasant thing to do. We don't like to think about things that threaten us or our loved ones, homes, or prized possessions being destroyed. Consequently, we tend to put off taking the necessary steps to protect ourselves and to reduce the potential for damage, injury, or loss of lives.

In the following chapters I describe how to protect your house from fire and how to increase your odds of escape and survive if you do have a fire. After reading this book, you'll be better prepared to prevent and deal with fire. Being prepared can be the difference between surviving or not.

 Fire Facts

Fire is the most common of all disasters and the easiest to avoid. According to the United States Fire Administration (USFA), every year in the U.S. there are approximately 2 million fires— from small ones to major conflagrations—reported to the local fire departments. That's 1 fire every 16 seconds, costing about $8.5 billion annually. Of these, 23% or nearly 500,000 are residential fires, costing about $3.8 billion in damages yearly.

Apart from property damage, annually fires cause about 4000 deaths and as many as 100,000 injuries with about 20,000 rated as serious. Most serious fire injuries are burns and smoke inhalation. Home fires account for the vast majority of deaths–3200-3600 or 80-

90%. Most fatal residential fires occur between 11 p.m. and 6 a.m., when people are asleep. Fires are especially deadly to children. Eighteen percent of all fire deaths are children under 10. Forty percent of fires that kill young children are started by children while playing with fire. The elderly are also frequent fire victims with about 900 older adults dying annually in fires. About 100 firefighters lose their lives each year while fighting fires.

Not Enough Oxygen

Contrary to popular belief, however, the primary cause of fire deaths is not being burned, as many think, but is by asphyxiation due to inhaling smoke or not getting enough oxygen. Remember, fire needs oxygen to burn, and consumes staggering amounts of it, thus diminishing the supply that people and their pets need to stay alive.

Tremendous Heat

A burning room is like an oven. On average, the floor level temperature is 90 degrees Fahrenheit, while at eye level the heat rises to 600 degrees, and a fully involved fire can produce temperatures as high as 1100 degrees. Heat generated by a fire can quickly overwhelm a person, making it difficult to run to get out, thereby increasing the chances of suffocating. Being in a fire is like being baked alive, even if you escape the flames.

Poison Gases

Smoke contains poisonous gases such as carbon monoxide, hydrogen sulfide, hydrogen cyanide, and sulfur dioxide. Exposure to such poisons impairs judgment and reasoning abilities, along with reduction of muscular control.

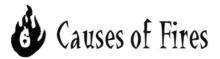 # Causes of Fires

People cause most fires. We do something stupid to ignite a fire, like smoking in bed, or we are negligent in periodically inspecting appliances and electrical equipment that could spark a fire. Take smoking, which is a major cause of house fires and the leading cause of fire deaths. Smoking is responsible for approximately 20% of all house fires. Plus fires caused by smoking are the most deadly, accounting for nearly 1/3 of all deaths. About 58% of all fires are set by smoking, cooking, children playing, and negligence in home upkeep, like overgrown brush, or not cleaning fireplaces.

Faulty Appliances

A major category of fires is caused by faulty heating or electrical equipment or from using this equipment incorrectly. Examples include overloading an electrical outlet or putting a heater too close to furniture or to flammable material or liquids. Together, these account for 24% of all house fires, with 14% due to heating problems and 10% for electrical equipment misuse or failures.

Arson

Another category of fires is incendiary or suspicious fires, such as when someone uses an incendiary device in an act of revenge or to fraudulently collect an insurance settlement. According to the USFA, arson is the third leading cause of residential fires and the second leading cause of death in these fires.

Fire Smarts Saves Lives

By knowing the major causes of fires, you can take steps to protect yourself and your home. For example, you can be more careful about where and how you smoke inside; you can be more careful when you cook; and you can caution your children and keep devices that could cause fires away from them.

Fire Inspect Your Home

Check heating and electric equipment regularly. This is a crucial step. Clothes dryers, for example, are responsible for about 14,000 house fires a year, according to the Consumer Products Safety Commission. We were one of these statistics. Our fire started when a 14 year old natural gas flex line leaked gas which erupted into flames.

 # Smoking

If you smoke, it behooves you to take basic precautions. We all know many of the precautions, they are self-obvious. Yet, we forget or think we're exceptions or don't pay attention and fires start.

Never Smoke in Bed

Don't smoke in bed or when you are lying down on a couch or recliner. You can easily drift off to sleep while you relax, and a fire can begin before you wake up. Due to the flammability of many furnishings and even some mattresses, by the time you wake up or the smoke detector goes off, the fire has often grown to deadly intensity.

Never Smoke When Tired

Don't smoke when you are very tired or have been drinking heavily. When you do, even if you aren't lying down, you can easily fall asleep, drop your cigarette, cigar, or pipe, and ignite a fire. Anyone who is excessively tired or has been drinking alcohol stands a much higher risk of dying in a fire because they take longer to become fully awake or capable of taking action, and they often use poor judgement, which compounds the situation. Excessive tiredness, alcohol, and drugs inhibit proper and rational thought processes.

Use Proper Disposal

Be careful when you dispose of your cigarettes, cigars, or pipe tobacco. Fires can start because these aren't completely out. For example, only use a large, flat bottomed, deep ashtray. Also, don't throw cigarette or cigar butts in wastebaskets or in garbage bags under the sink.

Make Sure it's Out

Make sure your cigarette is out cold. Dip it in a glass of water. Hold it under a running water faucet. Squeeze it in the palm of your hand. Be confident the item, whether it is a cigarette, cigar, contents of a pipe, or even a recently used match, is completely extinguished and cold before throwing it into the trash or placing onto any combustible or flammable material.

Designate a Smoking Area

Post No Smoking Signs.

Designate an area outside of your house or in a particular room a place one can smoke. Other areas become out of bounds. Have ashtrays in the smoking areas and nowhere else. Inform guests of where they can smoke and of your expectations. Be ready to step in diplomatically, such as to give your guest an ashtray or to politely direct them to the smoking area. You might even post "No Smoking" signs.

Kitchen Fires

Most kitchen fires start as a result of easily avoided mistakes like leaving pots on the burner too long, cooking on heat that is too high, leaving appliances running when not at home, or setting flammable items too close to the stove burners. Usually the fault lies in not paying attention or leaving the burners on when answering the phone, for example. Other times, we run out to make an appointment neglecting to make sure all appliances are off.

Turn Appliances Off

Make sure heat producing appliances, like toasters, toaster ovens, and coffee makers, are actually off by unplugging them when not in use, rather than depending solely upon the "off" switch. There could be a loose connection or a faulty indicator light so that even though it appears to be off, it is actually still capable of heating up and starting a fire.

Use Only Approved Appliances

Purchase only fully tested and accredited appliances that bear the label of a recognized testing laboratory such as Underwriter's Laboratories (UL) or Factory Mutual (FM). This means that the appliance has been subjected to, and successfully passed, safety and performance analysis by an independent lab.

Used Appliances

Before installing an appliance that you have purchased through a newspaper ad or at a garage sale, thoroughly inspect as much of the wiring that you can see, for fraying or cracking or other visible damage or wear. Also check the connections. Operate the appliance on all settings and leave it running for a while to make sure that it doesn't fail.

Appliances purchased from a recognized dealer usually come with a 30 day warranty. Ask the dealer if they have tested the appliance. Again, look for a UL or FM label before purchasing. Remember that older and used appliances, particularly ones in which you do not know the history and service frequency are a higher risk than new products.

Cook Safely

Stay in the kitchen while you are cooking. If you run upstairs, or go into the garden to get something you may get distracted and forget about the food cooking. Of course, sometimes the phone will ring or someone will come to the door unexpectedly and you must answer. When you leave, even for just a few minutes, you are taking a risk. It is common for people to have a poor concept of time, especially when involved in discussion, perhaps at the door or on the phone. Thirty minutes may only seen like ten minutes.

Set a timer or alarm in the kitchen that you can hear, or carry one if you must leave the kitchen while cooking.

A good way to keep time from slipping away when items are cooking in the kitchen is to set a timer or alarm in the kitchen, or carry a timer with you, if you must leave the room for a short period. Many stoves and most microwave ovens have timers that can be set to sound a signal after a predetermined amount of time. The less time you are out of the kitchen while items are cooking, especially items in the open such as on a stove or cooktop, the better.

Check Before Leaving

Always check the stove, microwave, hot plates, and other cooking appliances to make sure they are off before leaving the house, even if you have not been cooking. This is also a very good habit to develop doing before going to bed.

Flammable Objects

Keep the cooking area clear of objects that could catch on fire. Don't store flammable items, including food in boxes, paper towels, kitchen towels, on top of the stove or near it. And if your stove, hot plate or toaster is near a window, don't hang curtains or blinds.

Inspect Regularly

Make sure your stove and other cooking equipment are in good working order to avoid the chances of fire. Clean the filter in the exhaust

Combustible items should *never* be put on or near stoves or heaters.

hood, and duct over the stove on a regular basis. Check electrical connections to make sure they are tight and that there is no broken insulation.

Test Gas Connections

Test gas connections periodically at least twice a year and if you smell gas. Use a spray bottle with a mixture of water and dishwashing detergent—roughly a ratio of 1 part detergent to 10 parts water. Simply spray the solution onto the connections, and even all along the gas line between the wall and the appliance if you suspect a leak in the line itself, and look for bubbles. Escaping gas will create a bubbling effect. Should this occur shut off the gas supply and make repairs before using the appliance again.

Two men died in Texas while investigating a gas leak. After the residents had evacuated due to a strong natural gas smell, two neighbor men, who had training in commercial building security and evacuation procedures, entered the home in an attempt to find the leak. Moments later there was a tremendous explosion and fireball. Authorities determined that one of the men used a cigarette lighter in an effort to find the leak. **Never** test for leaking gas by using a cigarette lighter or any other flame.

Dress Safely

Be careful about what you wear when you cook, so *you* don't catch on fire. Avoid loose fitting clothing with long floppy sleeves and clothing made from flammable material, like party dresses or costumes with fur. If you have guests wearing such clothing in your kitchen during a party, caution them to keep away from the cooking area.

Spills Cause Fires

Keep the handles of pots and pans while being used turned to the rear of the stove and use rear burners for cooking when possible to reduce the chance of someone hitting them when walking by and spilling grease into the flame or onto the stove top, which could start a fire.

Use a Hot Mitt

In an effort to make sure no hot grease or other substances that could ignite come in contact with a flame or hot stove elements, use kitchen mitts or hot pads designed for kitchen use,

Pots and pans with handles facing forward can be knocked off causing spills, serious burns, and fire.

when picking up hot pans. Just as keeping pot and pan handles pointed toward the rear is important to reduce spill hazards, the use of a kitchen mitt will lower the chances of spills.

Responding to a Kitchen Fire

If grease or oil does ignite, never pour water on it. We all know that oil and water don't mix. If you add water to a grease fire it will spread the flames. Instead, quickly turn the appliance off. Then attempt to smother the fire by shutting the oven door if the fire is in the oven, or by putting a metal lid over a flaming pan. If these actions don't stop the fire and the fire is still not too large, use a fire extinguisher. If the fire extinguisher doesn't stop the fire, get out.

 # Kids & Fires

Ten percent of all fires are caused by kids playing with fire or by getting too near a fire. A key way to reduce fire hazards is to tell your kids about the danger of fire, so they don't take risks and play with it. The younger the child, the greater the potential danger. Educate your kids about the dangers of fire. Your cautions can keep your kids from inadvertently getting too close to a dangerous fire that can harm both themselves and the whole house.

Tailor the Message

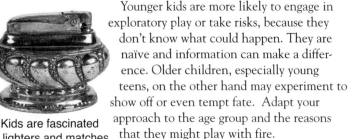

Younger kids are more likely to engage in exploratory play or take risks, because they don't know what could happen. They are naïve and information can make a difference. Older children, especially young teens, on the other hand may experiment to show off or even tempt fate. Adapt your approach to the age group and the reasons that they might play with fire.

Kids are fascinated by lighters and matches.

Keep Fire Away From Kids

Kids are curious and naturally drawn to playing with matches and lighters. They like seeing the flames pop up, like playing a game. Explain what could happen if they play with the matches and keep matches and lighters out of the reach of young kids. You might show them videos about fire made for children. Find out if their teacher plans a lesson on the subject. Maybe you can persuade the teacher or the principal to put on a program on home fire safety.

Keep Kids Away from Heaters

Never leave young children near fire or portable space heaters. Warn children to not go too near to heaters, even to get warm. Children move and jump around and can knock over a heater or fire screen or fall into a burning fireplace. Instruct children about the dangers of heaters and tell them to come to you if they need help in getting warm.

Discourage Playing with Candles

Warn children to never play with candles, just like they shouldn't play with matches. If you see your child with candles, take them away. If you allow teenagers to use candles to light up their room at night—and I advise against it—show them how to use candles safely. Always put out candles when leaving the room and when you go to sleep at night. Give candles plenty of clear space. Many

Keep candles away from kids.

fire departments recommend against candle use altogether due to the high danger of starting a fire.

Heaters & Furnaces

Fires started by heaters cause about 15% of all fires. So making sure your heaters are in good working order is another key step in avoiding fires. According to the United States Consumer Safety Commission electric heaters cause about 2400 fires yearly that cause about 80 deaths and 240 injuries with over $48 million dollars of property damage.

Replace Old Heaters

Older equipment is particularly dangerous because old wiring can be frayed or otherwise damaged, causing sparks that can ignite a fire. Older heaters can overheat and are prone to falling over, and do not incorporate modern safety devices such as "tip alarms" with automatic shut offs.

Portable heaters should have been tested and have a label on them from a nationally recognized testing laboratory such as Underwriters Laboratories (UL) or Factory Mutual (FM), or you should not use them.

Service Furnaces Regularly

Have your home furnace system inspected each year by a licensed heating contractor, and make any needed repairs. Proper maintenance prevents fires and carbon monoxide poisoning resulting from improper gas combustion.

The professional furnace service technician will inspect the furnace's flame, the venting system to assure it extends through the roof with no gaps or other deterioration such as rust or cracks, and that the furnace panels and grills are in place, and that the fan compartment door is closed and seals well. He may also use a device that can detect even very small amounts of carbon monoxide while the furnace is operating.

Change Filters

Homeowners and tenants should see that the filters, placed where the air returns draw in air for the furnace (found on ceilings and/or walls) are replaced annually or as often as needed. In cold climates the filters often need changing three or more times during a winter heating season. They need inspec-

Vacuum furnace
filters regularly.

tion and replacement as needed during the summer as well when forced air systems with air conditioning are used.

Clean Often

Floor and wall furnace grills should be kept clean of dust and debris by regularly vacuuming all accessible areas. It's a good idea to replace filters every fall just before the onset of winter.

Avoid Kerosene Heaters

Kerosene space heaters should be used indoors with great caution, and preferably not used at all. Electric space heaters with modern designed safety features are a far better choice. Unvented kerosene heaters, when incorporating modern design and properly maintained will operate at up to 98% efficiency, introducing little pollution into the indoor space. What people don't realize is that these heaters consume the air in the room. Air quality engineers recommend that kerosene heaters never be used for more than 2 hours at a time, and not at all in newer homes that have been designed to be air tight. Always open the window a crack in the room in which a kerosene space heater is in use. Some of the newer unvented heaters have sensors that automatically shut off the burner when oxygen levels in the room fall below a safe level.

Even the most efficient kerosene heaters must be used with extreme caution when children or elderly persons are present due to their greater susceptibility to pollutants. Because of their potential fire and health hazards modern electric heaters are a better choice.

Cool Before Refueling

Always let kerosene heaters cool before adding fuel. The danger is similar to what happens when you add cold water to a hot radiator in your car. It can erupt into hot steam and seriously burn you. Similarly the kerosene can explode when it comes into contact with hot parts.

Read the instructions and make sure that you know how to operate the heater. Always use only crystal clear "K-1" kerosene, not yellow kerosene, gasoline, diesel fuel or any other type of fuel in a kerosene heater.

Electric Space Heaters

There are many types of portable or space heaters. Radiant heaters heat objects in a direct line of sight in front of the unit, or they may have fans that more effectively spread the heat. Some heaters have heat elements, which are wires or coil like arrangements that become red and glowing hot when turned on.

Oil Filled Heaters

The safest space heaters are oil filled radiant units in which the oil sealed inside is warmed by electricity. Oil filled electric heaters usually have no fans or no exposed heat elements. Fire hazards of this type of heater are much lower than ones with heating elements, with or without fans. Whatever heater you choose, look for a UL or FM label.

Place in Safe Location

Never place portable heaters close to something flammable. Always place space heaters at least 3 feet from furniture and curtains and other flammable material like towels, clothing, and paper. Heaters placed too close to walls and doorways can pose a hazard. Flammable substances, which is anything that can burn, must be kept a safe distance from all heaters—including waterheaters. This includes solvents, furniture strippers, paint, fuel, soiled rags, glue, chemicals, paper, wooden items, and anything that can catch on fire.

Even heaters placed too close to nonflammable objects can cause the heater to overheat from improper airflow. The best rule is to not put anything within three feet of any heat device—be it a space heater, fireplace, or waterheater.

Make Sure It's Stable

Portable heaters can fall over and ignite a fire if there is a sudden movement, such as from an earthquake, kids or pets romping around, or a heavy wind. When purchasing a new space heater, look for one that has safety features such as an automatic shut off should the unit tip over or overheat. Select a heater that has a broad, flat base, so it is less likely to tip over. Some

Modern electric radiators are the safest space heaters.

heaters have an alarm that sounds when the unit is tipped too far over.

Furniture and boxes near heaters can ignite to start a fire. Be fire safe.
Always keep items at least 3 feet from any heat source.

Turn Off When Unattended

Never leave space heaters unattended. Don't go to sleep with one
turned on in the room.   While portable heaters may look quite safe, they
can overheat or fall over and cause a fire. The U.S. Department of Energy
and fire agencies recommend to *never* leave a portable heater running
unattended while you sleep and to never use one in a bedroom.

Never Plug into Extension Cords

Because space heaters draw a lot of current they should always be
plugged directly into the wall plug. Never plug a heater into an extension
cord. The high level of current it draws can overheat the cord, with
disastrous results.

 # Electrical Fires

Over 10% of residential fires are electrical related. When
the cause is faulty wiring within the wall it can be difficult to
locate the point of orgin of the fire.   There are a number of easy to
do steps one can take to prevent electrical fires.

Use Licensed Contractors

Always use licensed contractors when installing electrical wiring,
lighting or wall outlets. Contractors do charge more, but you are paying for
their expertise and know how. While you can save money by having a
handyman or your neighbor do the job, if a mistake is made it could cost
your home or your life. That's no bargain!

Use Halogen Lamps Carefully

Exposed halogen bulbs pose a high fire risk. Halogen bulbs operate at much higher temperatures than incandescent bulbs. A curtain hanging nearby can easily ignite, especially if it should be blown into the bulb. Fires can be started when a lamp with a halogen bulb is tipped over.

Always check that there is a bulb shield when buying a halogen lamp. Even with this safety feature it is wise to not leave the lamp on and unattended for extended periods of time.

Cover Plugs

Use plastic outlet covers to close outlets when not in use to prevent someone or something from coming in contact with live electricity. Children, for example, can stick objects into plugs when playing. Touching a "hot" wire can electrocute or seriously burn a person—and it can trigger an electrical fire.

Inspect Regularly

Periodically check your entire house. Be on the look out for loose wall outlets and malfunctioning outlets and switches. Feel lamp and appliance cords. Those that are warm to the touch, frayed or otherwise damaged are hazardous and should be replaced. Check extension cords for cracks or tears and replace any that even look suspicious.

Never Overload Circuits

Fuses that "blow" regularly are annoying. Many people get around this by replacing them with higher amp fuses, such as using a 20-amp fuse on a 15-amp rated circuit. Yes, you may avoid blowing fuses, but by doing this you defeat the purpose of the fuse which is to blow out when overloaded to cut off the power. Higher amp fuses may take longer to blow, which allows the wiring to overheat, often with disastrous results.

Always use correct the amp fuse.

Another common trick for preventing fuses from blowing out is to put a copper penny into the fuse holder. I have seen this short-cut countless times when inspecting buildings with fuse boxes. The coin permits a heavier and heavier electrical load as the wiring heats up. You never know there's a problem until a fire suddenly breaks out.

Signs of Circuit Overloading

- Lights dim when appliances go on.
- Heating appliances are slow to heat up.
- Fuses blow frequently.
- Circuit breakers trip frequently.

Extension Cord Safety

Use extension cords sparingly. If a wall outlet provides for two items to be plugged in, then plug in only two. Never use extension cords to run appliances that draw a lot of current. Too many items on one circuit can cause heating of the wiring of extension cords and within the walls. Circuit breakers may also trip and fuses blow under these conditions.

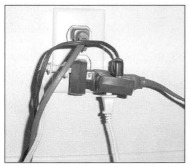

Too many plugs into one outlet can overload the curcit.

Use only modern extension cords. Inspect for cracking and other signs of age. If you notice any sign of wear, throw it out. Extension cords are inexpensive. This is not place to try to save a few pennies. Use extension cords with plastic protectors on the plugs so you can cover them up when not in use.

Keep extension cords away from foot traffic. Put them behind the furniture and don't run them under carpets or rugs where they can get damaged by being walked upon. Another danger is twisting extension cords around hooks or nails, which can result in tears and rips that expose the wires. Instead use brackets made for attaching cords to walls.

Use Proper Wattage

Avoid putting high wattage light bulbs into lamp fixtures. The higher the wattage the greater the heat it gives off, which may overload the wiring of the fixture and can also set lamp shades on fire or create a fire hazard to the ceiling onto which a fixture is attached.

Lamps and lighting fixtures have maximum wattage rating labels affixed to them. Most lamp fixtures manufactured in the US are made for bulbs of 60 watts or less. Look for the label. When there is no visible label to direct you, use 60 watts or lower blubs.

Unplug Malfunctioning Appliances

If an electric appliance shows any indication of problems such as giving off a burning smell, or smoke—unplug it. Simply turning it off may not be sufficient.

Look for maximum wattage label.

The switch may be malfunctioning so that it is not actually turned off. There may be a short in the appliance. If the cord is hot wear gloves or use a doubled up rag and unplug it imediately.

Give Plugs Room

Never push appliances such as refrigerators, dryers, microwave ovens, stoves, or furniture up against an electrical cord plugged into a wall receptacle. This crushing action can cause "conductive electrical heating" where the wire inside the wall heats up without tripping the circuit breaker or blowing the fuse. The result can be an electrical fire within the wall, which can take hours to start, perhaps after you have gone to sleep or have left the house.

A fire chief friend of mine told me of a two million dollar fire at the public high school that started just this way. A soft drink vending machine had been pushed against the plug in the wall. At night, when no one was there, the fire broke out.

Be Careful with Electric Blankets

Electric blankets and heating pads can overheat when covered with bedding or clothing. They are prone to being twisted, bent, and sat upon which can cause the wiring to become frayed, cracked, or come loose.

Electric blankets and heating pads that have been in service for some time or treated roughly should be replaced. Read the proper use and safety precautions before using. Never leave these devices running unattended.

Clothes Dryers

Clothes dryers must be used as carefully as are heaters. If the equipment doesn't function properly and fails to turn off when it should, for example, heat can build up in the dryer. Older dryers pose the special risk of gas leaks due to aging gas lines and connections.

Inspect Regularly

Make sure your dryer is in good working order by doing a careful periodic equipment check. Check the dryer venting for accumulated lint, and make sure the connections are tight and the venting tubes are in good condition, with no leaks.

Check Gas Line Connections

Check the gas line connection to make sure it is tight. For extra protection, use a thread-locking compound, which comes as a paste in a tube or can, and is available in hardware stores. The paste creates a tight connection that reduces the chance of the connections becoming loose as a result of the dryer's vibrations. Periodically check the gas line from the gas valve to the dryer and if it looks worn, twisted or kinked—replace it.

Vent to the Outside

Dryers should be vented to the outside of the building whenever possible. When venting to outside the building is not possible, as is sometimes the case in condos, apartments and some homes, vent the dryer into a self-contained lint control unit. Never vent a dryer into a crawlspace under the building or into a basement, attic or other such space.

Keep Flammables Away

The areas around dryers should be kept uncluttered and clean. Don't leave any paper, flammable liquids, matches, lit candles, or any other device that could start a fire or easily burn near the dryer.

Several years ago I conducted a loss control inspection for an insurance company in which a fire had destroyed a section of a beautiful home. My job was to determine the cause of the fire and make recommendations as to how to prevent such a loss from occurring again. As it turned out, the homeowner stored spotting solvents on a shelf over the washer/dryer—as many people commonly do without a second thought. This, of course, is a convenient place to keep items for removing or loosening stains and spots on clothing or other fabric items before placing into the wash.

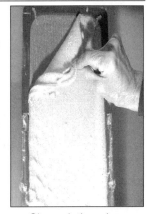

Clean clothes dryer lint screens before *each* use to avoid dangerous build up of highly flammable lint.

One of the containers was not properly closed after use; fell onto the floor near the dryer and the spill ignited upon exposure to the flame of the gas dryer. The result was many thousands of dollars of damage that could have been averted if the homeowner had realized the danger of keeping any flammable liquids near a dryer, including overhead cabinets.

Clean Out Lint Each Time

The grestest flammable is inside the dryer in the lint filter. Lint is extremely flammable and can readily ignite from a spark or even high temperatures. Clean the lint screen regularly to avoid dangerous build-up.

Never Operate Unattended

Just as it is foolish to leave space heaters running unattended, don't operate the dryer when not at home or after going to bed. The fire that burned my home down was started by the dryer in the garage. After my wife loaded the dryer she went back into the house and only 15 minutes later the whole garage and much of the wood shake roof of our home was engulfed in flames, all due to a leak at the gas supply connection to the dryer. Had we been asleep we may not have escaped alive.

Install New Gas Lines

Gas dryer lines, called "flex lines," flex only so far, then they crack when bent any further. Moving the dryer involves disconnecting and reconnecting the gas line, which can result in a leak at the connections or gas valve.

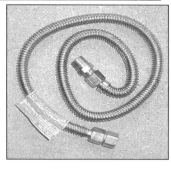

Replace the flex line that connects the dryer to the gas outlet when purchasing a new dryer or moving your dryer to a new location. Leaks can occur at small cracks caused by moving the appliance. In fact, the movement itself can loosen gas connections so that gas escapes. The dryer's flame can ignite such escaping gas. Remember the old adage: better safe than sorry. It's safer to replace the gas line.

Flexible Gas Hose can become cracked or loose and leak gas leading to an explosion.

🔥 Fireplaces & Woodburning Stoves

Fireplaces provide attractive lighting and ambi-ance, as well as warmth. We all enjoy sitting around a fire—toasting marshmallows or "roasting chestnuts on an open fire"—as the song goes. Fireplaces and stoves must be used safely.

Woodburning stoves are commonly the souce of heating many parts of the country, especially where winters are cold and wood is plentiful. Nonetheless, they are dangerous and cause over 9 thousand residential fires every year. There were two in my home in Montana when we moved in, but I disconnected them and have never used either. Why? Two reasons. They are a fire hazard and a safety hazard for young children and the elderly due to the extreme heat they generate.

Routinely Clean Vents and Flues

Make sure fireplaces and woodburning stoves are in good working order before using. Chimneys and stovepipes should be professionally inspected each year, as recommended by the National Fire Protection

Association (NFPA). When used regularly, inspect every 6 months and after every three cords of wood burned.

Clean flues and chimney venting to remove build up and obstructions so that the smoke goes up the chimney and not into your house. Periodic cleaning is vital to remove built up creosote, which is an oily by-product of burning wood. Creosote sticks to soot and ashes to build up in chimney vents and stovepipes and can erupt into flames when there's a fire burning.

Clean stovepipes and chimneys regularly to clear out cresote buildup.

Use Fireplace Screens

A mesh screen or glass fireplace enclosure prevents sparks from flying out of the fireplace into the room. A properly fitting glass fireplace enclosure, which is preferred, reduces heat from being sucked out of the house and up the chimney. Glass enclosures allow the enjoyment of the fireplace and reduce heating costs while lowering fire danger.

The average volume of air pulled through an open chimney in an hour is equal to twice the total volume of air in your house. In fact, more heat is lost through a fireplace opening than through an equivalent size hole in the wall.

Burn Only Hardwood

The type of wood burned determines the amount of heat generated, degree of creosote buildup, and amount of ash. Softwoods, including pine and Douglas Fir as well as artificial logs, produce the highest level

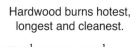

Hardwood burns hotest, longest and cleanest.

of creosote. Seasoned or slowly dried wood is better than green wood. Hardwoods such as cedar, mesquite, almond, and oak burn hotter, slower and leave less ash while producing fewer deposits of creosote.

Dispose of Ash Wisely

Make sure the ashes are thoroughly cool before disposing of them. Make sure there are no hot embers still lingering. Always place ash in a metal container with a lid. Just to be safe, never leave containers inside the house or other structures. My great Aunt Cecelia, who used her fireplace regularly, worked her ash into planting beds and her garden. If you have a cabin, it is tempting to dump ashes outside somewhere in the woods. This is unwise because embers can ignite dried grass and grow into a full fire.

Install a Chimney Cap

Without your being aware of it, sparks and burning embers can fly out of your chimney and land on your roof, that of a neighbor's home or into nearby trees and bushes. This is particularly hazardous if you have a wood shingle roof or live in a wooded area. Chimney caps keep out rain, leaves, varmints, birds, and bird droppings that can clog the chimney.

Minimize the Danger

Fully extinguish fireplaces and woodburning stoves before going to bed or leaving the house. Keep flammable objects away from fireplaces and wood stoves, just as you avoid putting objects near heaters and dryers. The general rule of thumb is to maintain at least three feet of clearance, and I see nothing wrong with five feet or more. In particular, keep matches, flammable liquids, and piles of newspapers and wood away from the fireplace or stove, since the heat or sparks of a fire can easily ignite these materials.

Jake, a friend of ours routinely dried logs on top of the woodstove in his get-away cabin. Even more foolishly Jake often stoked up the fire—just before leaving the building. He felt safe in doing so, since the fire was contained within the stove. One day when returning after a 20 minute walk with his dogs he opened the door and could see nothing because the room was black with smoke. A huge fire burning on top of the woodstove. In a panic, Jake grabbed burning logs and ran out the door. After opening up all doors and windows miraculously there was no damage—but only because he'd gotten home soon enough. A few more minutes and the burning logs would have fallen on to the floor and the cabin would have been history!

Woodburning stoves create a wonderful romantic ambiance but pose a high risk of fire.

Insurance companies typically add around 2% to a homeowner's policy to compensate for the inherent hazards presented by wood burning stoves. Without question, they are a wonderful source of inexpensive heat, as compared to propane, natural gas, and electricity, but the potential danger is very real and not worth the risk.

Don't Burn Trash

Never burn trash in your fireplace or woodburning stove. Doing so can damage your chimney and create a safety hazard. The colored ink from comics and newspaper becomes a toxic vapor when burned and can infiltrate the living area and adversely affect your health.

Small amounts of newspaper are often used to help get the fire started. This practice is generally safe as long as the amount of paper is only enough to get the wood started on fire and it is placed directly under the wood and not near the entrance to the fireplace or wood stove. Never use the colored newspaper sections—even as a starter.

Light Fireplaces Carefully

When lighting a gas fireplace, always strike the match *before* turning on the gas. The danger in turning on the gas first is that too much gas can come out, creating a bigger flame than you expected when lighting the match.

Fireplaces and woodburning stoves should contain only small to moderate amounts of wood and a small amount of paper or other kindling material. BBQ lighter fluid, kerosene, gasoline, or any other type of flammable liquid should never be used to start a fireplace or woodburning stove.

Candles & Kerosene Lamps

Light from candles and kerosene lamps provide a wonderful subdued ambiance, ideal for a romantic or festive touch. But they must be used with considerable care because the open flame can ignite a fire and turn a party into a disaster.

Secure Well

Always put candles and fuel burning lamps in a secure non-combustible base, on a level, sturdy surface. Be sure the lamp or candle is away from the wall and other objects. Heat from the open flame can slowly heat the wall's surface, causing it to catch fire. Don't tempt fate. Keep the flame at least 3 feet away from the wall, so that a gust of wind or the heat generated by the fire cannot heat the wall. Check that candles and lamps are sufficiently far away from shelves, the ceiling and hanging objects, like curtains and towels that could catch fire should the flame flare up. Put your hand over the candle or lamp to feel the heat. If your hand feels too hot, leave a little more space—just to be safe.

Never Leave Unattended

In seconds a fire can start from an open flame. Fuel burning lamps are particularly dangerous because should one topple over, the fuel can spill and catch fire. Never leave burning candles or kerosene lamps unattended. Stay in the same room with burning candles and lamps at all times. Never go to sleep while candles or kerosene/ oil fueled lamps are on. Fuel should always be stored as you would other flammable liquids—preferably in the garage.

Keep Away from Pets and Children

Be especially careful when using candles and burning lamps around children because they are prone to knock them over while playing. Instruct children on the dangers of open flame lighting and remind them of the dangers when using. Be a good model to your children by handling candles and burning lamps safely yourself.

Keep pets away from burning candles and lamps. Cats tend to climb up onto shelves and can knock something onto the candle or lamp. Keep puppies and exuberant dogs a good distance from burning candles and fuel buring lamps.

Globes on oil lamps are extremely hot.

Use Appropriately

For light during power failures, battery powered lights are far more safe than candles and fuel burning lamps. Never use a candle to light up a closet while searching for things. Use a flashlight instead. Don't walk with burning candles or lamps because you might trip.

Trim wicks to 1/4 inch and extinguish candles when they burn down to within two inches of the holder. Kerosene and oil fueled lamps have adjustable wicks that can be moved up or down to adjust for brightness. Don't adjust the wick up to the point where smoke is created. When finished using the lamp, turn the wick down until the flame is extinguished. Don't move the wick back up until you intend to relight the lamp. When lighting, expose about 1/2 inch of wick, light with a match, and replace the glass cover. Remember, even though the actual flame of these lamps is contained by the covers, the glass becomes very hot so the three foot principal should still be used.

Camp Lighting

Candles and kerosene lamps designed for home use should not be used when camping. When camping use only lamps and lights specifically designed for camping purposes, and then with care, following the manufacturer's instructions and warnings. Camp lights and cooking units should be kept at least 3 feet from any combustible materials. Flammable liquids and propane cylinders should be kept at least 20 feet or more from any camp lighting or cooking equipment.

Tiki Torches and Bug Candles

Tiki torches are commonly used in yards during the summer barbecues and evening events because they create a wonderful festive setting. The traditional kind have open flames.

Open flames always require attentiveness so it does not come in contact with trees, bushes, fences, buildings, or party decorations. Extinguishing Tiki torches is similar to that of candles in that they can be snuffed out by the user by removing their oxygen or put out with water. Make sure they are completely out before moving them back inside the garage or other storage area.

Candles for use in the yard, often called "Citronella Candles", are used to keep bugs away. The same precautions should be used with these candles as with candles used inside the home.

 Barbecues

Barbecues are a fun way to cook when used safely. There are two types of barbecues. The original type burns charcoal briquettes which are saturated with lighter fuel and lighted with a match. A second type has lava rocks and is powered by propane or butane gas. These are lighted by striking a match or an igniter button, opening the valves and the gas is dispensed from a Liquefied Petroleum Gas (LPG) tank.

The gas ignites sending out a flame to heat the rocks. Take the same precautions you would when cooking on a kitchen stove when using the barbecue.

Position Securely

Always be cautious when using a portable barbecue. Remember it holds a semi-open fire. Although the fire is inside the barbecue, flames can flare up when the lid is open. Position the barbecue several feet from shrubbery, patio furniture, and hanging objects. An open green lawn, concrete, cobblestones, tile, or other substances that can't catch fire are good locations. Notice I said "green lawn". Toward summer's end lawns become dry and brown, and can easily burn. I know this because just recently my next-door neighbor did just that. It burned low and slow and eventually to trees near the house and become a nightmare.

Barbecues are often used on decks and balconies without any problems. Nonetheless, to be safe, put the barbecue on a protective base made of a nonflammable, non-combustible material such as sheet metal or concrete.

Keep Guests and Kids Away

Keep family members and party guests, especially when serving alcohol, from getting too close to the barbecuse. Always keep kids at a safe distance. When a guest is cooking, light the barbecue yourself, and then turn it over to the cook.

Check occasionally to make sure that the cook is handling the barbecue safely. When needed, give safety suggestions in a gentle, helpful way so that the festivities are balanced with a dose of caution.

Party Safely

Barbecuing is often the central activity at yard parties where people are decked out in festive outfits. Don't wear loose clothing that can brush against the cooker and catch fire. Keeps guests wearing draped or flowing clothing away from the cooking area. When serving alcohol keep an eye on guests, who may have overin-dulged. They could bump into the cooker and knock it over or catch their clothes on fire.

Keep Tools Handy

Keep a set of tongs for manipulating the hot coals within easy reach. Always take care that the coals don't fall out. If a coal does fall from the cooker, quickly grab it with the tongs and put it back into the barbecue.

Keep a fire extinguisher nearby so that if anything does catch fire you can quickly put it out. In the yard, a garden hose is always a good choice to have readily available. Remember though, that if the fire is of grease origin, don't apply water—use the fire extinguisher. If you set something like the lawn on fire, or other items such as the paper plates, towels, or a bush, the hose will do an effective job.

Use Correct Lighter Fluid

Use only lighter fluids designated for use with charcoal barbecues to light the coals. *Never* substitute gasoline or any other flammable liquid. After applying the appropriate amount of lighter fluid, replace the cap and place the fluid container a safe distance from the cooker. Do not set the lighter fluid next to the barbecue. Never use starter fluid on a fire or on hot coals.

Use only lighter fluid designed for BBQ's. **Never** use gasoline.

Operate Gas Barbecues Safely

Read—and make sure you understand—all the manufacturer's instructions before using a LPG fueled barbecue. Pay particular attention to the warnings. The gas is contained in a pressurized steel cylinder that has the explosive potential of several sticks of dynamite.

Periodically check propane barbecues for gas leaks. Spray a soapy solution of water and dishwasher detergent on the hoses, connections and tank. If bubbling is observed, close the valve at the LPG tank and call a repairman. Never use a match to check for leaks.

Watch for Dripping Grease

Meats such as chicken, especially with the skin on, can drip substantial amounts of grease onto the coals or rocks. That grease can ignite and flare up and burn the cook and nearby people. Excessive amounts of grease may also drip all the way down, past the coals or rocks and pour onto the ground or onto the propane

tank or propane fuel line. As the grease is very hot and propane is highly flammable, it is recommended that drippings that escape the barbecue be caught in a metal container before they can drip onto the propane tank, lines, or onto the ground.

Shut Down When Not in Use

After you finish cooking on a charcoal barbecue, cover with the lid to prevent flare-ups. Shut down propane barbecues by turning off the gas valve, which will shut off the supply of gas from the tank.

Be especially careful when cooking on a gas barbecue.

Close down open barbecue pits used at campsites or the beach by dousing with water or covering with sand or dirt.

Always check to make sure all the coals are completely out. To do this, tap the coals with a tongs and turn them over. They should be completely black without any light reddish glow, which indicates that the coals are still smoldering and could flare up again, which is particularly hazardous when it's windy. Double check by putting your hand a few inches over the coals to check for heat. If you feel any warmth emanating from the barbecue, douse the coals with water until they feel cold to the touch.

🔥 Gasoline & Solvents

Be especially careful when using gasoline or other flammable liquids needed to operate equipment. There is always a danger of igniting a fire when refueling equipment, as well as when even moving or storing them.

Don't use gasoline or other flammable liquids for purposes other than those for which they are intended, such as cleaning floors, because doing so could produce friction and static electricity that can become a source of ignition. The slightest spark, a match lit at the wrong time—even a static-electric discharge can result in fire or explosion. Be aware, too, that ordinary materials, like clothing and rags, can become flammable when soaked with oil and grease.

Cool Before Refueling

Add fuel to equipment, such as mowers, chainsaws, snow blowers, or edgers, only when the devices—especially the manifold—are cooled down. The exhaust manifold is usually the hottest

Refuel outdoors away from structures when the equipment is cool.

part and is where the exhaust exits from the engine. Often there is a muffler and sometimes a spark arrestor as well. When gasoline or other fuels come in contact with a very hot surface, such as the exhaust manifold, muffler and surrounding parts, the fuel can explode.

Work in Well-Ventilated Area

Perform refueling in an outside area open to the air. Don't refuel in a garage or carport. Make sure you work sufficiently far enough away from any structures so that they will not become exposed to the flames if a fire does break out. In an open area, you can isolate a fire and prevent it from spreading.

Prevent Spills

Use a funnel to add gasoline to power equipment to avoid spilling. Wipe up spills, then move at least 10 feet from the fueling location before starting the motor. Gasoline vapors can travel along the ground and be ignited by a nearby flame.

Never Clean with Gasoline

Gasoline and flammable liquids, like lacquer thinners, acetone, and methyl ethyl ketone (MEK), lighter fluid, make great solvents for cleaning ceramics, glass vases, car parts, floors, and the oil drippings in driveways. Using fuels to clean is dangerous. Flammable liquids should be used only for the purposes indicated on the container labeling—and then with caution.

When I was a boy, a neighbor badly burned his hands and arms while cleaning oil stains from his driveway. He was using a scrap of old woolen blanket material and gasoline to do the job. The scrubbing action caused a reaction that ignited the gasoline in the rag and on his hands.

Not only are fuels and solvents flammable, but some pesticides are also highly flammable and need to be stored and handled with considerable care.

Never Smoke Around Gasoline

Never smoke when using flammable liquids. We all know this, of course, but how easily we forget or figure it's only for a moment. A spark, ash, or just the heat from a cigarette can ignite fuels and lead to a disaster.

Store Safely

Keep flammable liquids in well-secured containers with the lids

tightly closed. The best containers are usually the originals used when purchasing. Otherwise use only approved safety containers that carry a designation indicating that it is approved for use by a fire safety authority. If there is no safety stamp on the container it is

Keep flammable liquids in closed containers and store properly.

probably not safe for storage of flammable fluids.

Don't Over Stock

Keep the amount of flammable materials stored around your home to a minimum. It is wise to estimate the amount of fuel needed for gasoline-fueled household equipment, like lawn mowers and edgers, for the next 2 months, and keep only that amount on hand. If you need more, fuels are readily available at local hardware stores and gas stations.

Many municipalities set a limit on how much gasoline can be stored at a residential location—generally about 10 gallons—and specify how it must be stored. Ten gallons is probably way more than most of us would use in a number of years. When it comes to having gasoline around, less is better.

Store Outside

Never store flammable fluids hear a water heater, kitchen stove or any other heat source. Instead, store fuels outside in a cool, well-ventilated area, out of direct sunlight. A storage shed separated from the main house is a good choice. The next best storage site is in the garage. If you live in an apartment, use an outside area for storage, such as a storage locker in the garage. If you don't have a safe storage place, it's better to purchase the products as you need them, rather than risk a blow-up due to unsafe storage.

Throw Out Oily Rags

Never pile oily rags or rags soiled with paint thinner up in the corner or under the sink. Don't put them into containers that can easily burn, like cardboard boxes. Chemical reaction, called spontaneous combustion can cause the rags to suddenly ignite without a spark. Lack of air circulation creates a dangerous chemical stew. As the heat rises, the rags can erupt in flames.

Instead, dispose of soiled rags in metal containers with tight-fitting metal lids. Commercial businesses, like gas stations put soiled rags in metal containers with foot-operated lids. Stepping on a lever opens the lid so you can throw in soiled rags, and then automatically snaps shut when lifting off your foot.

 Holiday Safety

The holiday season, running from Halloween to New Years, is a time of joy and good feelings. It is also a time of increased risk of accidents—especially fire. Most fire losses during this time of year are preventable. Knowledge, preplanning, and simple preventative action is all that is required.

Christmas

It's easy to get carried away with festivities and forget to pay attention to safety during the holiday season. Chistmas and New Years are times to take special precautions, especially when children are around. When everyone is in a festive mood and liquid spirits are flowing freely, decorations and candles can be knocked over. Leaving holiday lights burning unattended is an invitation for accidents and tragedy.

The United States Fire Administration reports that each year there are an estimated 12 thousand fires causing over 80 million dollars damage and approximately 250 injuries and 40 deaths during the three days of Christmas—December 24, 25 and 26. Even if you don't celebrate Christmas personally, celebrations are all around. Take precautions to be fire safe.

Fire Proof Trees

Something in the range of 33 million live or cut natural trees are sold for Christmas celebrations. Nearly one third of the households in America bring a tree into the house at Christmas time. Fire resistent tree sprays are available that can be applied to make a Christmas tree more resistant to fire. Flocked trees generally have flocking that contains a fire retardant, but that does not make the tree completely safe. Keep in mind, no tree is fire proof. Artificial trees and greenery are fallable and can burn, too. When choosing an artificial Christmas tree, make sure it is labeled as fire-retardant.

Use Lights Safely

There is something magical about a tree decorated with lights that takes us back to being a wide-eyed child, with visions of sugar plums. Lights put off heat that can start a fire. Don't overload the tree with lights. They can put out too much heat which will excessively dry the tree, even if it is in water, and drastically increase the chance of fire. A lot of lights can overload circuits, too. Generally, a couple strings of lights about 12 inches or more apart is best. Use reflectors on large bulbs to direct heat away from the limbs. Don't drape crisscrossing networks of lights around a tree. Doing that can concentrate too many lights in one spot, thus focusing the heat generated by the bulbs.

Inspect Lights First

Inspect electric lights before hanging them on the tree or around your yard. Insulation wrappings should be unbroken, with no visable or bare wires. Check each bulb connection to be sure that it is tight. Examine the connection points at either end of the string of lights. They should look solid, as when new and never appear loose or worn.

After the tree is decorated, check lights every day or two to make sure they are still in good condition. It's also a good idea to recheck after holiday parties and when children have visited to make sure none have been knocked out of position.

Use Correct Lights

Make sure the lights you use are correct for that use. When placing lights indoors, use either lights designed for indoor use only or those described as for "indoor/outdoor" use on the box. When using lights outside, select lights labeled for exterior use, since these have additional protection against the outside elements.

Turn Lights Off

Turn tree and other indoor decorative lights off when you go to sleep or leave the house. Put outdoor lights on a timer so that they can stay on at night as a neighborhood display and turn off automatically when the sun comes up in the morning. It's best, however, to turn off outside lights when sleeping at night and when away from home because hot lights drapped on shrubbery, which may be dry and flammable, can ignite.

Never Put Candles on Trees

You may have seen candles on trees in movies and illustrated in history books. The sight of a tree with dozens of small burning candles instead of electric lights must have been amazing. The famous author, Robert Lewis Stevenson's wife was fatally burned when her robe ignited from such a candle-lit tree. Never attempt to decorate a tree with candles. Keep candles a safe distance from trees and decorative boughs laid out on mantles and in table centerpieces.

Hang an Extra Smoke Detector

Place the tree in a location that is several feet away from any heat source and that does not block an exit. Put a smoke detecting ornament on your tree. These life saving decorations will detect smoke in the proximity of the tree. Alternatively, mount an ordinary household smoke detector on a nearby wall or above the tree.

Water your tree and discard it properly.

Water Trees Daily

Christmas trees dry out quickly, making them more prone to ignite when exposed to heat from holiday lights. The drying process can be slowed by putting the tree in a pan with water and replenishing it daily. Even better, is a self-watering tree stand, which has a small reservoir of water in its base but needs regular refilling, too. Big trees use up to 5 gallons of water a day.

Make a Fresh Cut

When the tree is cut in the forest, sap flows to the base and the base also dries out somewhat, sealing off the tree at that point. Make a fresh cut at the bottom of the tree trunk just before putting the tree into water. Even when you make the cut just before placing into the pan or other water container, you must put the tree into the water as soon as possible, preferably within a very few minutes, or the tree will again begin to seal itself off and will not be able to effectively draw up water. The result will be a tree that will dry out faster than one that can drink the water effectively.

Also make sure the container of water the tree is sitting in never dries out. If it does, the same drying and sealing action will take place and the tree will not be able to drink as well from that point on.

Dispose of Trees Promptly

When the holiday season ends get rid of your Christmas tree and other holiday plants promptly. Needles get so dry that they fall off with the slightest movement. Pointsetta leaves get stiff and dry. Take these trees and plants to the curbside for special pick-up, if available, or to the local dump. Don't let old trees and plants lay around in your house, because such a pile of dried trees and plants makes good kindling for a fire—especially when kids are around.

Fourth Of July

Irresponsible use of fireworks results in damage to property amounting to over 36 million dollars annually. Most Americans enjoy celebrating with fireworks, but responsible use is a must. Many areas have have banned possession and use of fireworks by the general public, which has reduced property damage, brush fires, and injuries. Most areas allow the use of Class C fireworks by the public, a less lethal version of the Class B fireworks like those that we see at professionally staged shows. Responsible use of this potentially very dangerous product is of prime importance.

Read the Instructions

Read all instructions and warnings on each and every firework product — every time—before using them. Don't assume you know how to shoot the thing off. Take the time to review the precautions. If there are kids around, be a good model for them. Read the instructions out loud to them and discuss mistakes they could make and what could happen.

Keep Fireworks Away from Kids

Keep all fireworks out of the reach of children. Be extremely cautious when using these devices in the presence of children. When I was 16 years old, and should have know better, I attempted to make a bigger firecracker than could be purchased at the fireworks stand. Everything went well for the first few I made, but through a simple mistake I ended up blowing part of a couple fingers off, nearly blinded myself and ended up in the emergency room. Fireworks, like automobiles, and baseball bats must be treated with appropriate caution, and only by those old enough and capable of understanding and heeding the safety directions. Kids get excited by the festive atmosphere and when they find fireworks, they are likely to try to set them off. Thousands of kids have been blinded and lost hands by fireworks that have blown up too soon.

Fireworks are beautiful and dangerous.

Discard Properly

Douse used fireworks in a bucket of water before discarding in the trash. Treat used fireworks like you would treat cigarettes and cigars. Make sure that they are fully extinguished and disposed of properly.

Halloween

Each year in the U.S., between October 30 and November 1, fires cause nearly $60 million in property damage, 30-40 deaths and over 200 injuries.

Use Retardent Materials

When purchasing cos-
tumes and masks, make sure
they are labeled "flame-
retardant". Use only
flame-retardant materials
in home made costumes,
made out of bed sheets and
other common fabrics can be
quickly consumed by
Be fire safe! flames if ignited. Be sure
Use flashlights, to read and follow laun-
not candles in dering instructions because
jack-o-lanturns. special laundering procedures are required to retain
the fire retardent properties.

Use fire retardant cloth and paper when setting up haunted
houses and displays. Never use dry leaves, gauze, styrofoam
(polystyrene foam), paper, or other combustible items. Once
started, a fire in materials, like piles of leaves, spreads rapidly.

Use Battery Lights, Not Candles

Jack-o-lanterns with a lit candle inside that flicker to make
its eyes twinkle is synomous with Halloween. Without them
Halloween isn't the same. The danger, however, is obvious—
especially when kids in flowing costumes are carrying them
around. Eliminate the danger by using a small flashlight inside
the jack-o-lantern or a liquid light that will glow for hours after
the light stick is bent and activated.

Smoke Detectors

Forewarned can mean the difference between getting out of
a burning building alive and being overcome by smoke and
flames. Smoke detectors are the first line of defense against being
hurt in a fire. When smoke is present the detector goes off,
sounding a shrill scream, alerting you that a fire is burning
somewhere near. Early warning is the critical key to getting out
of a burning building alive and unharmed.

Mount Throughout the Home

Our house was built in the 1970's when smoke detector requirements were minimal. Our one detector was located on the ceiling at the top of the stairs. Had there been a series of interconnected smoke detectors, with one in the garage, we would have received an earlier warning, making our escape much easier. In our case, the fire burned through the wall and the roof had been fully engulfed before our detector went off. We were aware of the fire before the detector activated.

Our new home has 12 smoke detectors and 3 carbon monoxide detector/alarms. Even if you do not interconnect all the smoke detectors together, having several, placed throughout the house, including garage, unfinished basement, and even the attic provides the early warning system that can be the difference between life and death.

Where to Place Detectors

Put a smoke detector in every major room including the garage, basement and workshop, if you have one. Even put one in the attic so that it can be heard throughout the house, especially during the quiet of the night. Most important is putting one just outside every sleeping area. It is best to sleep with the door closed since a closed door slows the fire's progress, giving extra protection. For this reason it is wise to install a second detector inside the bedroom. On floors without bedrooms, place smoke detectors near living areas, such as living rooms, dens, and family rooms. Hallways longer than 30 feet should have one mounted at each end.

Mount detectors on the ceiling, at least 18 inches away from dead air spaces near corners and where the ceiling joins the wall. Alternatively, mount them on walls at least 12 inches below the ceiling and away from corners. Place the detector as high as possible, within the above-mentioned limits because smoke rises.

Never place smoke detectors within three feet of air registers, or exterior wall doorways or windows because drafts can impair the detector's functioning. Don't mount detectors on uninsulated exterior walls or ceilings because the batteries can be affected by extremes in temperature. Never paint a smoke detector because it can hinder its function.

Smoke detectors are the first line of defense.

When it comes to carbon monoxide detectors, there should be at least one on each level of the home and in the basement. They do not work well in garages as they will be regularly set off by the exhaust of automobiles.

Types of Detectors

There are two types of smoke detectors and some variations among them, such as detectors with a light that goes on when the unit activates. there are detectors for the hearing impaired with features such as flashing lights and louder alarm sound.

Ionization Smoke Detectors

Ionization Smoke Alarm

The most common type of smoke detector is the small plastic ionization unit that fastens on the ceiling or wall. It functions by using an ionization chamber with two metal plates and a source of ionization radiation to detect smaller amounts of smoke from flames. When smoke enters this chamber, particles in the smoke attach to the positively charged ions and neutralize them, causing the current to stop flowing between the plates, which triggers the horn.

Photoelectric Detectors

The second type of smoke detector is the photoelectric detector, which detects smoky fires, such as a smoldering mattress. It is a small rectangular or round plastic box with a light source on one side. On the other side is a photo-detector located an inch or two below where the light beam would normally strike. In normal smoke-free air the light beam goes straight across the unit so that the photo-detector doesn't register anything. But when the air is smoky, the smoke particles disrupt the beam, scattering the light waves, which triggers the alarm.

Use in Combination

Because the ionization and photoelectric detectors detect different fire conditions it is advisable to install one of each on every dwelling level. An ideal approach is to alternate the ionization and photoelectric detectors from room to room. The advantage of using both detectors is that the ionization detector reacts more quickly flaming fires, whereas the photoelectric detector reacts more quickly to smoldering fires.

Problems with Battery-Operated Detectors

Battery operated smoke detectors are excellent devices provided they are properly maintained. People are the weak link in the system. Too often we forget to replace the batteries. Another problem is that when units frequently sound off from kitchen cooking, for example, people dismantle the detector to keep it from sounding.

Other times people smoking, especially when they shouldn't be, such as conventioneers smoking in a nonsmoking hotel room, dismantle the smoke detector in the fear that their smoke will trigger it and bring the management. Obviously dismantling the smoke detector is foolish because it cannot do its job.

Carbon Monoxide Detectors

Carbon Monoxide detectors alert occupants to dangerous CO levels. Carbon monoxide is a by-product of incomplete combustion which can occur with furnaces, water heaters, stoves, and other fuel burning devices, and during a fire. Never run a generator indoors, including the garage, because CO can build up quickly. It is known as the "silent killer" because it has no odor. Whole households have perished from a slow build up of CO inside the home.

Hard-Wired Detectors

Hard-wired detectors are wired right into the building's electrical system, just like ceilings lights or doorbells. Some systems have a back-up rechargeable battery in case the electrical system fails such as during a power outage or a fire. A hard-wired system works year after year without the problem of having to change batteries.

Hard-wired systems can be wired in such a way that all the smoke detectors in a building are linked. Then if a fire breaks out in one part of the house, such as the garage, the alarms ring throughout the house and not just in the area where the fire has broken out.

Choose a hard-wired system with a battery backup, so the smoke detectors will keep working if the power fails, which often occurs shortly after a major fire breaks out. Installing a hard-wired system in an existing house requires an electrician to install new wiring into the walls that can be expensive and may not be feasible. On the other hand, when doing a major remodeling or when rewiring your home, adding a hard-wired system is easy and adds minimally to the cost. The same is true when constructing a new home.

Detectors with a Light

Some detectors come equipped with an emergency light that turns on when the detector's alarm sounds. During a fire the main power of the house often goes out. The advantage of a unit with an emergency light is that it helps you find your way out of smoke filled rooms that are *very* dark—even during the day time. When we had our fire, the electrical panel on the side of the garage was quickly melted by the fire causing all the lights in the house to go out. Since we only had one smoke detector with no battery backup and no emergency light, we were in total darkness, stumbling down the stairs and groping around to find the deadbolt key to unlock the front door to make our escape. Had we had the system I incorporated into the rebuilt home we would have had enough illumination from the detector's emergency lights to move quickly and safely down the stairs and find the key. Even though the light is of low illumination—it can make all the difference in aiding your escape.

Good for Hearing Impaired

When someone in your family is hearing impaired, installing smoke detectors with flashing lights and an extra loud ring is essential. There are several million hearing impaired people in the U.S. alone who may never know a smoke detector is trying to warn them of imminent danger.

Test Monthly

Test all detectors—whether battery operated or hard-wired—monthly to be sure they are still working properly. All you have to do is to press the "self-test" button. If it is working, the detector will give out a loud beep. Replace the batteries at least every 12 months—preferably every 6 months. Some smoke detectors use lithium batteries, which are claimed to be good for up to 10 years. Don't trust that claim. Replace the batteries anyway. New batteries are cheap insurance. Replace batteries immediately when detectors make a beeping, popping, or squeaking sound every few minutes. This sound is a sign of low power.

The National Fire Protection Association recommends that the smoke detector unit itself be replaced every ten years to insure that you are fully protected against worn out parts. However, replacing detectors more often may be needed. If you notice any damage to the detector when doing your monthly check—replace it. Why take a chance?

When testing the detector and changing batteries, take the time to clean cobwebs and dust from the units. Smoke detectors are sensitive instruments and their ability to function properly can be impaired by dust.

🔥 Fire Extinguishers

Fire extinguishers are the second line of defense in battling fires. But to be effective it must be readily accessible so you can grab it quickly when a fire erupts. If you lose precious minutes searching for the extinguisher the fire can grow out of control with disastrous results.

Ratings

Extinguishers are rated as A, B, C or ABC. The "A Class" rating indicates the extinguisher can put out fires with ordinary materials like burning paper, wood, cardboard, cloth and many plastics.

A "Class B" rating means the extinguisher can quell fires involving flammable liquids, such as oil, grease, gasoline, kerosene, lacquer thinner, paint thinner, solvent based paints, acetone, MEK (methyl ethyl ketone), and other solvents.

A "Class C" rating means the extinguisher will extinguish fires of energized electrical equipment, such as appliances, switches, electrical panel boxes, electrical power tools, hot plates, and toaster ovens.

A "Class ABC" extinguisher has contents that are effective on all three types of fires. The primary ingredient in ABC type fire extinguishers is a substance called *monoammonium phosphate*. They do not contain water. The dry chemical, when sprayed from the fire extinguisher onto the fire removes the oxygen, thus putting out the fire.

Capacity

For Class A fire extinguishers, the number that precedes the letter "A" represents a water equivalency. For example, 2 represents 2 1/2 gallons of water and a 3 represents 3 3/4 gallons of water. There is no water in this type of extinguisher, but the rating is a "water equivalency" rating since water will put out Class A fires.

For Class B & C fire extinguishers, the number that precedes the letters represents the number of square feet of fire the extinguisher can extinguish. For example 10 represents 10 square feet, and 20 represents 20 square feet. The ABC type of extinguisher is effective in extinguishing a variety of fires, which is reflected in the three letter classifications.

How to Choose

A good choice for general home use is a "2A-10B:C" rated fire extinguisher. A 2A-10B:C extinguisher will put out most residential fires confined to a small area. The numbers indicate the extinguisher's capacity and size of the fire it can put out. The letters indicate the types of fires the unit is effective in putting out. A 2A-10B:C is a good choice because it is reasonably priced and of a size that most people can operate. However larger units are available to handle larger fires.

The rating indicates what kind of fires the extinguisher will quell.

Always check that the fire extinguisher is "listed" and "labeled" by an independent testing facility such as UL (Underwriters Laboratory) or FM (Factory Mutual).

Where to Place Extinguishers

For ultimate protection mount a fire extinguisher in each room. Most important is having one in the kitchen and in the garage, where most home fires start. If you have a limited budget, place extinguishers in alternate rooms. At a minimum, keep at least one fire extinguisher on each level of the house, plus one in the kitchen, basement, workshop area, and garage.

How to Position

Position extinguishers so they are easy to reach when a fire occurs. Choose a visible location on the wall or on an easy to reach shelf. It is better to affix the extinguisher to wall than it is to set it on a shelf or counter. When mounted on a wall you know where it is in an emergency, whereas when not affixed it could get moved. If a fire breaks out, you can lose precious time searching for an extinguisher that has been moved or gotten covered with stuff. In fact, commercial fire codes require that extinguishers be affixed to a wall.

In the kitchen, place the extinguisher on a wall or shelf near the stove or other cooking equipment—but not too near. Heat from cooking can reduce the extinguisher's effectiveness, or cause it to fail altogether. Mount the extinguisher at least 10 feet away from sources of heat, such as a stove, fireplace, or heater. Yet it should be close enough that it is in easy reach if a fire breaks out. If the kitchen is small, post the extinguisher in a nearby area easily accessible—and visible —from the kitchen, such as in the hallway just outside.

Check Regularly

Fire extinguishers gauges are usually near the top of the unit, just below the handle. The gauge shows the amount of charge, or pressure within the unit. Extinguishers vary slightly as to how the indicator conveys the message that the unit is still fully charged or needs recharging, but they are designed to be simple to read. Check the gauge every month or so to make sure the indicator is still in the "OK", "Charged", or green area.

Fire codes generally recommend extinguishers be checked and recharged annually by a professional servicing company, which can be found in the yellow pages usually under "fire extinguishers". Many new fire extinguishers come with service tags on them, and they nearly always have a tag on them after being serviced. The tag has a written date, or a month and year punched out. Either way, the extinguisher should be checked and serviced by the expiration date on the tag, at which time the servicing company will put on a new tag with new date.

When doing your self inspection, if the dial indicator shows "discharged" or is in the red zone, it will not perform properly and should be serviced immediately. Sometimes you will find extin-guishers on sale and purchasing a new one to replace the old is less expensive than having your old one serviced.

Practice

All extinguishers are operated in the same basic way. The safety mechanism is released when the pin is pulled off. Then the extinguisher should be aimed at the **base** of the fire. Squeezing the handle discharges the contents. Use a sweeping motion while spraying.

Make sure to read the instructions before the practice opera-tion. Follow the instructions as to how far from the fire you should stand when attempting to put out the flames. This is especially important because with some fires, such as flammable liquids, oil and grease fires for example, if you activate the extinguisher when

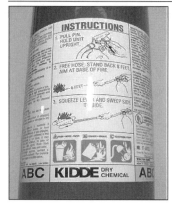

Acquaint yourself with how to use your extinguisher. Don't wait until an emergency to read the instructions.

standing too close you will simply spread the fire rather than extinguishing it.

Being in a state of fear and panic at seeing a fire erupt, people often grab an extinguisher and move too close to the fire. The blowing pressure of the extinguisher can actually spread the fire, making it worse. On the other hand, if the user has practiced following the instructions, a small fire can be easily put out with a hand held extinguisher.

Brief Everyone

Everyone in the house should practice operating the fire extinguisher. One approach is to review the instructions with family members and provide a demonstration. Then have each person try it. Fire personnel are usually happy to provide pointers on how to operate extinguishers. Most fire departments offer periodic public demonstrations at the fire station and some   have a demonstration video available for loan.

Use Caution

A fire extinguisher is only useful when the fire is small and confined to a small area—a few square feet, such as a fire on a kitchen stove top, in a trash can, a small burning bush, or in the corner of the garage. If the fire grows beyond that area, stop using the extinguisher and head out of the building to safety.

A small fire can be smothered with a blanket or sand or doused with a bucket of water. Be cautious about the type of fire so as not to apply something that may spread it, such as throwing water on an oil or stove top grease fire. People have been badly burned while using flour to try to smother a stovetop fire. When such fine dusts are combined with just the right amount of air an explosion can result, burning anyone nearby.

🔥 Security Bars

Many homes and apartments have security gates and window bars to keep out bad guys. The problem is that during a fire, the bars can imprison you in a burning inferno. Many people have died needlessly because of being unable to escape through a window because of security bars.

Dangerous

Death as a result of being unable to escape through windows with security bars has become so common that most U.S. cities have enacted laws requiring that at least one window in each bedroom have a quick release mechanism on the window bars. The release mechanism enables the bars to swing open when you press a lever.

Replace Unmoveable Bars

I have personally seen hundreds of homes and apartments with window bars bolted to the exterior walls, with no quick release features. I have visited sites where children and even entire families have died because a fire occurred in another portion of the premises while they were asleep in the bedrooms and were unable to escape due to blocked egress. If there are security gates or window bars on your home that don't have quick release mechanisms, *replace them.*

Sometimes you can find a mechanism that can be attached to older bars and gates. Generally, however, trying to rig a release mechanism is harder than simply replacing the window bars in the bedrooms. The units are not too expensive and considering the dangers of the old fashioned fixed units, the small cost and time to do it is well worth it.

Fixed security bars turn a bedroom into a potential death trap in a fire.

If you don't own the building, ask the owner or manager to replace fixed window bars on bedroom windows and locking security gates at exits to the property. If the owner is not cooperative or procrastinates, you might call your municiple building department to get information on the ordinances regarding security bars and present this to the owner. If they continue to stall, you may have to press the issue by filing a habitability complaint with the code enforcement division of the building department.

Make sure to make demands upon the owner in writing and keep a copy. In some cases you will be permitted to have the bars replaced and can deduct the cost from your rent. Check with local authorities and your attorney before doing this.

🔥 Alarms

Having smoke detectors and fire extinguishers is a must for every home—no exceptions. If your budget allows, you might look into other life safety products such as installing a fire alarm. The third line of defense is an alarm system with central station monitoring that automatically notifies the fire department of fire and smoke.

Central Station Monitoring

Central station monitoring is a feature of professionally installed alarm systems. When the alarm is triggered by fire, smoke or a burglar break-in, the computer that runs the system grabs

your phone line and calls a central monitoring station where a live person is standing by 24 hours a day to call the fire or police department. In some areas, especially smaller towns and rural areas, alarm calls go directly to the fire department or police.

Most systems permit you to change the length of time between the triggering of the alarm and the call to the monitor. If it is a false alarm

Modern alarm systems notify you of fire and break in tell you where the problem is.

caused by something burning on the stove, for example, you have a brief window of about 45 seconds to call the central station and abort the call to 911 dispatch.

Identifies Kind of Emergency

Computers that operate professional alarm systems can distinguish between an alarm for a fire and a break-in, as well as where in the house the forced entry has occurred. Some systems can detect leaking water such as from burst pipes. They come with sophisticated battery backups that will take over and keep the system running in event of a power failure.

Professional alarms can be expensive, but they are not as expensive as you might imagine. Once installed, they operate for years with little maintenance or cost. The monthly monitoring service is less than most people pay for cable TV and well worth the cost. Not only can it save your life and the lives of your family should a fire start during the night, for example, but also it monitors when you are away from home.

Avoid False Alarms

False alarms cause the fire and police departments to respond unnecessarily. Most cities charge a substantial fee after the first false alarm. While they will never acknowledge it, the monitoring service or 911 dispatch may place a lower priority in responding to an address where there have been many false alarms. Furthermore, the ringing alarm is quite loud and false alarms upset neighbors who run out to see what caused the alarm to ring.

Professional fire alarms are more reliable than passive smoke detectors. For one thing, the system detectors, which are hard-wired, have no batteries that beep and tempt us to dismantle the system.

Causes of False Alarms

False alarms are usually triggered by everyday activities like cigarette smoking. False alarms are most commonly caused by food burning on the stove. They can also be caused by cobwebs or spiders getting into the alarm's smoke detector, which is why it is important to periodically vacuum the detectors. Air canisters used to clean dust from the inside of computers work.

During my years working in loss control, I heard numerous stories from clients who had to pay fire and police departments for false alarm calls, many of which were for systems that not only were capable of detecting smoke and fire, but also intrusion, and had the sensitivity of the motion detectors set so high that the systems were activated by cats or even mice.

Train all Household Members

False alarms can be prevented by making sure that everyone in the household knows how to cancel the alarm's call to the central station before they call 911. The alarms have a keypad that is mounted at the main entrances, such as the front and back doors. Punching in a special code—which has been programmed into the system—within 30-45 seconds cancels the distress call. However, the call alone is not sufficient. Typically, you must tell the monitor a special "secret" number or word that identifies you as a person authorized to cancel calls. Finally, you must have the phone number to call the monitoring center readily available.

Usually there isn't enough time to locate your roll-a-dex to look up the monitoring station phone number. Often, people paste the central station phone number on the side or bottom of the phone—but not the secret code. All of this may seem easy. However, the alarm's siren, bells, and horns are very loud and piercing. It is disorienting. It is best to set off the alarm and to have each household member experience the distress the wailing alarm causes and practice aborting it by calling the monitoring station. Most services recommend periodically testing the fire alarm by spraying it with a substance they supply which triggers the alarm.

🔥 Emergency Lighting

Smoke filled rooms are dark—*very dark*. Panic combined with coughing from smoke and you have a deadly situation. When our home burned down we had the most deadly combination of all—smoke filled rooms and no house lighting because the electrical panel was affected by the fire, resulting in a total shutdown of the system.

Light Saves Lives

Having even a dim light can make the difference between life and death. Don't depend upon normal household lighting because the electrical system can short out and cease to function, especially in a serious fire when you need it the most.

Smoke detectors with lights are a good start. Keep in mind though that if the smoke detector is not a battery power unit or a wired in unit with battery backup, you won't have the benefit of the detector's emergency lighting if your house power fails.

The vast majority of smoke detectors sold in the U.S. have no built in lighting system. Even though the detector light on those so equipped is dim in comparison to a professional emergency lighting system, it just may be enough to help you and your family see your way out.

Commercial-type emergency lighting units are about the size of a shoebox, can be installed in residences, and consist of high intensity floodlights. They are usually attached to the wall, near the ceiling in hallways, large rooms, and near the exits. They operate off batteries that are constantly recharged by the main electrical system and turn on automatically when the power goes down.

Placement

Ideally, you should place emergency lighting units in each room, but at least along main corridors leading to exits, and at the exits. If the central power to the building fails the emergency lighting will turn on and light the pathways to the exits from your house — usually the front door and back doors. If you live in a condo or apartment with only one exit door, consider having the lights lead to that door and also to a large window on the opposite side of the apartment from the front door. This way there is light to an alternative way out if a fire prevents getting to the door.

 # Sprinklers

Automatic fire sprinkler systems activate and begin controlling a fire before the fire department arrives. Those precious ten to twenty minutes can mean all the difference between minor damage and complete destruction. Often sprinklers totally extinguish the flames and they almost always slow the spread of the fire until the fire department arrives.

Sprinklers Reduce Damage

Sprinklers can contain fire quickly so that damage from heat and smoke is greatly reduced. Insurance companies and other fire experts in the field claim that sprinklers decrease fire damage by as much as two-thirds compared to homes without them.

Having a sprinkler system in your home offers additional protection against being injured by the fire or the deadly smoke and gases. Had there been an automatic fire sprinkler system in my home when the fire occurred, damage would have been very limited as far as fire and smoke. Of course, we would have had water damage, but our lives would not have been endangered as they were and we wouldn't have lost so many uninsured precious contents, including irreplaceable family mementos.

Sprinkler head can be recessed to hide from view.

Should a fire start when no one is at home, an automatic fire sprinkler system will spring into action.

Variety of Models

Some fire sprinkler systems activate the sprinkler heads only in the vicinity of the fire, which minimizies water damage. Usually sprinklers systems are tied into alarms systems which call the central station monitor if there is a water pressure drop in the fire sprinkler system. Still other systems have sound detectors that use built-in microphones placed around the building to detect unusual sounds, including fire, bursting water pipes, and even strong winds that might cause damage.

About 90 percent of fires in homes with newer sprinkler systems, where the sprinkler heads operate independently, are contained by just one sprinkler head, thus reducing water damage. Sprinkler heads come on, one at a time, as they are activated by the fire's heat. Sprinklers are not activated by cigarette smoke, or smoke occasionally created in normal kitchen cooking operations. The probably of an automatic sprinkler system accidentally activating and spraying water because of a manufacturing defect has been estimated at approximately one in sixteen million.

Installation

Installing fire sprinklers in an existing home is complicated and generally impractical for most homes. However, when installed during the construction of a new home sprinkler systems cost only about one and one half percent of the total construction costs, which is about the cost of carpeting. This small investment can greatly reduce the damage of a fire and increases the home's value. Insurance companies often offer lower premiums for homes equipped with automatic fire sprinkler systems.

When adding an addition to your home, consider including a sprinkler system. Sprinkler heads no longer need to extend down from the ceiling or out from the walls. They now can be mounted flush, so all you see is a flat round disc that can be painted the color of the ceiling or walls, and pipes can usually be hidden. Check that the contractor who installs a sprinkler system adheres to National Fire Protection Association (NFPA) codes and standards, along with local fire safety regulations.

 Defensible Space

Most house fires start inside the home. Fires that start outside can ignite your home. If you live in a bushy or wooded area or if your yard is over grown your home is at risk. Fortunately there are simple actions you can take to vastly reduce the chance of your property and contents sustaining fire damage due to outside forces.

Create Defensible Zones

Defensible space is an area around a structure where fuels and vegetation have been treated, cleared or thinned out to slow the spread of a fire towards the structure. It provides room for firefighters to work unhampered.

Defensible space is divded into concentric "Zones". The idea is to reduce the potential fuel in defined areas radiating out from your home to make it is easier to defend. Zone 1 is a 15-30 foot area— preferably 30 feet if you have the room—measured from outside edges of the building's eves. This area should be cleared of flammable vegetation around every structure.

In Zone 2, which extends 75-125 feet beyond Zone 1, vegetation should be thinned out by removing diseased, dead, and stressed plants and pruning trees and shrubs. Plant trees and shrubs in Zone 2 at least 10 feet apart and don't let them grow over 10 feet in height. Increase these distances if the trees and shrubs are on a slope.

Clusters of shrubs under trees can help a fire to spread from one plant to another as well as set fire to a tree. Large clumps of plants also make it harder for firefighters to get good access around your house. It's better to keep plants in smaller clustered groups to make it easier to get by them should a fire break out.

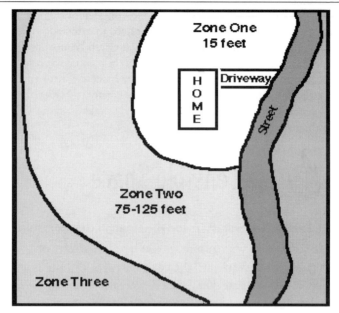

Defensible Space Zones

Keep Vegetation Away from Propane Tanks

As part of the defensible space plan, all grass and weeds should be eliminated from propane tank storage areas. It is essential to do this whether the tanks are inside an enclosure or not, and no matter how far the tanks are away from structures.

Keep Trees Away From Buildings

Trees are a fire danger. Overhanging branches can fall on your house if the tree burns. Trees shed dead leaves and drop needles on your roof. Ideally, the distance of a tree from the house should be greater than the height of the tree—when full-grown. If trees are closer than this guideline, trim them to be safe. Make sure no limbs overhang the roof and that no limbs are within 10 feet of the chimney. When planting a tree, take into consideration how tall it will grow at maturity.

Plant trees away from buildings.

Plant Fire-Resistant Plants

Avoid planting hedges in Zone 1. Instead cultivate fire-resistant plants in this vital area. These include: oleander, rockrose, and ceanothus. Some resist fire because their leaves are high in moisture, and some have leaves with low oil content. Cactuses and succulents, which tolerate heat due to their high moisture content, are a good choice. While other plants dry out during hot summer, succulents remain, well—succulent and therefore resistant to fire.

An alternative to decorating with plants is using non-flammable materials, such as bark-mulch, rock, and gravel. Use fire resistant materials for fences, patios, decks and other structures in Zone 1.

Highly flammable plants are more likely to catch fire because they have dry leaves, high oil content with woody stalks and plenty of air space to fan the flames. Don't plant bamboo, sugar gum and blue gum eucalyptus, juniper, scotch broom, and decorative grasses near your home. Dig up Algerian ivy, which is flammable and has a tendency to take over. Ask your local nurseryman to show you fire-resistant plants. There are many beautiful varieties from which to choose.

Cactuses and succulents are fire resistent.

Clear Regularly

Clear out dry dead leaves or branches at least once a year. Not only do they look unsightly but they burn easily. Even fire resistant plants can get over grown and throw off dead leaves and branches. Don't allow these too accumulate. Once dead, fire-resistant plants lose their resistant properties, such as moisture, and burn just as readily as other dried brush.

Have a Hose Ready

Hook up a hose that is long enough to stretch around your house and to nearby structures on your property. If there is only a single water outlet, attach a single long hose to it. Where there are more outlets, attach hoses long enough to reach all areas of your house. It's preferable to have more than one hose-ready outlet in case you can't get to one outlet, you can use another outlet. More hose-ready outlets might enable you to spray the fire with a few hoses.

Use Spark Arresters

When clearing dry grass and brush use spark arresters on the mufflers of gasoline-powered mowers, edgers, and chain saws.

Make sure to check the muffler regularly because hot gasses from defective mufflers can ignite dry grass, weeds, or brush.

Install Screen Vents

Burning embers from wildfires can enter houses through attic and foundation vents and ignite the house. Install wire mesh screens over all attic and foundation vents. Screens of one half inch or smaller size are generally recommended.

A mortician I knew in Seattle who worked the night shift, heard unnerving scratching and clawing sounds when he got home each morning. After weeks of trying to locate the sound, he called a handyman for help. The scratching and clawing sounds were discovered to be birds, who had gotten through the wide openings of the roof vents, and were making nests in the attic. Screening the attic vents helps to keep burning embers from entering, while also keeping birds and other creatures out.

 Yard Safety

We usually don't think about yards as being fire dangers. Yet, many fires start in wood piles and sheds, then spread to your home. With just a little effort you can identify fire risks lurking in your yard and correct them.

Store Firewood At a Distance

The image of firewood stacked up against the side of a house conveys a certain sense of security. There's plenty of wood to keep us warm over the winter. Actually firewood stacked near your house is a hazard. If it catches fire, so will your home. Store firewood away from the house. Never stack it against the building. Besides risking a fire, wood stacked against your house is an invitation for termites.

Place Sheds at a Distance

The same rule of thumb for distancing trees holds for placing sheds and other outbuildings. Ideally the distance of an outbuilding from the house should be greater than its height. If there are existing outbuildings that are close to the house, take extra precautions. For example, you might attach a water hose close to the building to be able to wet it and the surrounding area, should a fire start near it.

If you have a shed for storing firewood, keep it neatly stacked. Keep dry leaves, weeds or brush from entering into the shed. Have a tight fitting door that will keep kids out.

When placing outbuildings, such as a shed or greenhouse employ the

Debris against your home is like having a pile of kindling waiting for a match to ignite it.

distance to height principle. When looking for a new house use the principal to assess fire risk of prospective properties that you view.

Keep Lids on Trash Cans

Trash cans are often kept close to structures and in garages. Fires originating in trash cans cause thousands of house fires every year. These can be from someone not fully extinguishing a cigarette and throwing it into the trash, to someone intentionally setting the stuff in the can on fire, to spontaneous combustion from someone not properly disposing oily and solvent soaked rags.

Overflowing trash cans are much the same as a big pile of kindling. Trash provides fuel that fires can quickly consume, generating huge amounts of heat to ignite nearby structures.

Keep the lids on trash cans at all times to reduce oxygen available in the can. Fire requires substantial amounts of oxygen—the more oxygen it can get the hotter and larger the fire. Keeping lids on trash cans helps contain the fire. Metal trashcans are the best from a fire standpoint. Commonly used plastic cans melt easily, producing toxic fumes, and can even add to the fire, depending upon the type of plastic used by the manufacturer.

Enlist Neighbors

When you reduce the fire danger in your surrounding neighborhood, you help to protect your house.

Talk with neighbors about safety hazards you notice on their property, such as tall trees that could fall on your house. You might gently advise them how they can protect their own house, which will benefit you as well. Most neighbors will appreciate the information since it helps them protect their houses.

Notice Fire Hazards

Notice overgrown trees and bushes on city property and request a clean-up crew to trim and clear them.

Dried leaves are flammable.

You may need to trim branches that overhang your property yourself. Contact the city or county beforehand because they might do it at no charge.

Post Street Number Clearly

If the fire department is delayed even by a few minutes while trying to find your house in an emergency, the situation could easily go from bad to worse. Clearly post your address in a prominent location so firefighters can find you in event of a fire. Fire codes require builders and homeowners to put their street address in a prominent location, such as on a post at the street, on the mailbox stand if there is a mailbox at the sidewalk, or on the front of the home. It also requires that the letters be at least 3 inches high and of a color or of a reflective material that can easily be seen by firefighters from the street.

🔥 When to Flee

When a fire becomes too big to fight you must flee from it. You must protect yourself as best you can if you can't get out of the building to survive with as little injury as possible. Ability to make quick judgments is essential. As a rule of thumb, a fire is considered out of control if you can't put it out within 30 seconds with a fire extinguisher, water, blanket, or other means. It's time to *get out!* Fire departments generally recommend getting out of the building at first sign of fire. If you aren't sure if you should flee, always err on the side of safety and *flee!* When in doubt, get out!

When is a Fire Too Big to Fight?

Fires often occur at night—like the one that destroyed our home—when families are asleep. Don't count on having time to congregate and evacuate together. Basic fire safety knowledge combined with staying calm can be the difference between surviving or succumbing to a fire.

Feel the Door First

It is generally recommended that you keep your bedroom door closed when sleeping because closed doors slow fires. If a smoke detector sounds or if you hear someone shouting: "Fire!" *don't open the door* because a wall of flames may greet you. Instead, touch the door with the back of your hand to feel its temperature. When the door is warm or hot to the

Feel the door with the back of your hand.

touch, the fire is right outside the door, it could flare up into your face as the rush of air from the room when you open the door feeds the fire. If it is cool, it's probably safe to open. Be cautious and open the door slowly because you don't know what's on the other side.

Lean on the Door

Lean on the door as you open it, with your face pointing away. Leaning on the door will enable you to quickly slam it shut if there is pressure from fire and excessive heat on the other side. Lean against the door so it won't push too far open if there is fire on the other side, open it a crack to see what you will be facing. Be ready to slam the door shut fast, should there be an onrush of flames

Lean on the door while opening it slowly.

Make A Run for It

You don't want to get trapped in a blazing hallway. Be very cautious about to *where* you are running. Make sure that the fire is far enough away before running into a hallway to make a run for. It is easy to get disoriented in the smoky light. People often run right into the fire and become trapped. Fires move fast and can surround you in a few seconds.

If you decide your best chance is a quick run, be mindful. Run out and away from the flames. Always close doors behind you to slow the progress of the fire. Stay low to keep below the rising heat and smoke. It will be cooler and less smoky closer to the floor. Call to others, especially children, and tell them to run away from the fire and out of the building.

Try to grab something to protect you from flames. Wrap yourself in blanket or carpet or wall tapestry, or drapes before making run for it. If your protective wrap catches on fire, drop it and continue to run away from the flames.

What to Do When Trapped

Always try to get out first and hide only when there is no way out. If you are trapped, you've got to try to survive until you are rescued. The rule of thumb is to stay as far away from the fire, heat, and smoke as possible. Make sure to discuss and practice what to do if trapped needs to be addressed during your family meetings—where to go, and what to do to increase your chance of survival.

Find an Air Source

Most fire injuries and deaths result from smoke inhalation, not having been burned. Gaining access to air increases survival chances. If there is a window, position yourself by it. Open the window—and breathe. If the window opens at the top and bottom, open the top and bottom slightly so rising smoke will go out on top and fresh air from outside will be drawn in through the bottom.

Climbing out onto the roof where there is fresh air. Attracting attention from that position might be the best action to take. Beware, however, that you could fall through the roof as the interior of the home burns.

If you can't get out of the window, try to attract attention Scream and wave something out the window to attract attention so that rescue workers will see you. Wave a white cloth, a towel, or *anything* handy. Hang a sheet outside the window, for example. If there's nothing available, take off your shirt or other clothing and wave it out the window.

Get to a Bathroom

A bathroom is generally the safest place to be, especially if it has a window that can be opened. When trapped in a building, get to a bathroom. In a bathroom you can fill the sink, bathtub or shower with water, or even use the water from the toilet to protect yourself.

Close the bathroom door and keep it closed. Wet towels and place them along the bottom and sides of the closed door to slow the smoke and flames from entering as well as help to keep the oxygen in the room. Look in the medicine cabinet for adhesive tape. Tape the cracks around the top and sides of the closed door to further maintain your oxygen supply within the room and to keep out the smoke.

Make sure there is a roll of adhesive tape in each bathroom. It's inexpensive and a roll lasts for years. Most first aid and emergency kits include adhesive tape. If yours doesn't, get some.

Seal yourself in.

Keep Down Low

When there is no window and you can't get to a bathroom, the next alternative is to get down low where the most air will be. Get under the heaviest furniture in the room to protect yourself from falling objects. The lower you are, generally the better. As smoke and heat rises, getting to a lower floor—even the basement—is often the best solution.

Avoid Closets & Attics

Never hide in a closet where the risk of being overwhelmed by smoke is very high. Clothing hanging in the closet is especially vulnerable to burning and engulfing you. Burning fabrics and plastics in buttons, belts, and shoes is toxic and can kill.

Never try to hide in the attic. Kitchens may also be deadly because of gas appliances and plastics often found there. For the same reason, garages are generally not recommended because of flammable liquids. An exception might be when if you could drive a vehicle through the garage door or the side of the garage wall.

# Escape-Ready Home

An escape ready house helps you to get out of it fast when you must make a sudden exit. This applies to fire as well as other emergenices when you and your family members must leave the building quickly. Having objects placed on stairs, landings, along hallways or other pathways leading to a safe exit from the home can slow your progress, especially if you have lost electricity and are trying to maneuver in near total darkness.

Have an Escape Plan

When you have a plan and have practiced carrying it out, you don't have to think during a crisis. You know exactly what to do and where to go. Our homes seem very familiar and it is hard to imagine having trouble getting out. Just as a test, try blindfolding one of your house members in a variation of Blind Man's Bluff and timing how quickly they escape. It could be fun and could provide a tangible way to help children understand the problems they face during a fire.

Analyze your house and identify all means of escape from each room. Generally escape routes are from a room to a hall to an exit. Make a floor drawing of your home and, in a different color such as in red, draw the escape route from each location. If you live in an apartment identify the escape route from your door to outside of the building. This is particularly important if you live on an upper floor of a large building.

An "escape ready" house will help you get out of it quickly. One of the easiest and no expense approaches is to keep corridors and stairs free of objects that could keep you and your family from getting out quickly. For example, don't have large bulky decorative pieces in the corridors. Make sure kids don't leave their toys by their doors or in the hallway. Clutter hinders efficient emergency egress as well as being a fire hazard itself.

Identify Alternative Exits

Stand in each room and identify all of the ways of getting out of it. Look for a second escape route from every room. If there is a window, check that it can be opened wide enough to climb out. Discuss with each family member how he or she would get out of the window. If it is high from the ground and needs a ladder, make sure each person knows where the ladder is stored—which should be nearby—and how to use it.

Clear Corridors

Clear out corridors and stairs of objects that could hamper someone from getting out quickly. Move furniture away from entrances to corridors. Teach kids to put their toys away and not to leave them in doorways, on stairs or in the hallway. You might even role-play with them what could happen if someone tripped on a toy carelessly left on a stair or in the hall. Kids love play-acting. Opening up your corridors is the single most important step you can take right now. It's easy and costs nothing, yet pays off big in added safety.

Get Window Ladders

If your house is multi-storied be sure there is a clear way out from the upper floors. Attach a window escape ladder to the window. Typically ladders come in two sizes. A two-story ladder extends to 12 feet and a three-story ladder extends to 23 feet. Ladders that extend up 50 feet can be purchased online or ordered through fire supply stores. Two and three story ladders hold up to 600 pounds and are made with strong plastic or metal steps. Some of the longer ladders have a capacity rating of up to 1000 pounds. They have sturdy handles that fit over windowsills. Keep the ladder near the window, and in case of a fire, the handles can be quickly thrown over the sill to climb down.

Some people connect two or more ladders together to make a longer ladder. This is workable provided the ladders are securely fastened together, and you don't exceed the capacity rating with too many people on the ladder at one time. Be sure to test the connections by subjecting the ladders to a pull of several hundred pounds to make sure they will hold together.

Making a home escape ready involves addressing all the elements that could slow or even prevent safe exiting from the building. Smoke detectors are a must and each step you take, makes your home safer to live in and easier to exit from in an emergency. Be sure that if you have security bars on windows and gates for the doors, they have quick release mechanisms to allow fast egress.

Ladder hooks over window sill.

Fire escape ladder

Fire Drills

Thinking clearly is difficult when fleeing a fire because of panic and confusion. This is natural. A few seconds wasted in hesitation can be the difference between getting out unharmed and becoming trapped in a deadly situation.

An ounce of prevention
is worth a pound of cure.
—Benjamin Franklin

The "Great Escape" is an annual event held in early October in communities throughout the United States during Fire Prevention Week. It was inspired by the popular story about a cow that knocked over a lantern in Mrs. O'Leary's barn setting off the Great Chicago Fire in 1871. About a million families take part in Fire Prevention Week activities. According to the President of the National Fire Protection Association, what families learn in the Great Escape saves more than 40 lives a year because people know what to do if a fire breaks out.

Discuss the Plan with Everyone

Hold a household meeting to review the plan of action during a fire. Make sure to include borders, babysitters, household workers like cleaning ladies and gardeners, along with guests and even neighbors, if they are interested. Discuss how to fight a fire. Make sure that everyone knows where the extinguishers are mounted, how to get them off the rack and use them.

Discuss when to stop fighting a fire and get out of the building instead. Spell out specific steps for escaping each room, describing which way to go to the hall or to get out the back door, for example. Talk about what to do if one gets trapped. You might pose "what-if" scenarios and brainstorm how to best handle it. Plan on about an hour for a meeting, and have these meetings regularly, generally once or twice a year and when newcomers move in. Everyone being fully prepared for the worst case is being fire safe.

Practice, Practice, Practice

Practice is necessary so everyone's reactions become automatic under the high-pressure, hot-house atmosphere of a fire, that can rapidly get out of control. Practice helping family members to be calmer in the face of grave danger, to act rationally, much like a fireman, airline pilot, racecar driver, or police officer

Practice getting under something large and sturdy.

is trained to respond quickly, yet remain calm. Family members will respond calmly when they have confidence that they know the proper procedures and can act automatically to take the best action in the face of a fire.

Conduct regular fire drills at home. Place family members in various areas of the house. Make sure that each person knows how to escape from his or her location. It's particularly important that children understand what to do. Then ring the smoke alarm and start the drill.

Role Play

Have each person act as if it were a serious fire—the big one. For example, they should yell "Fire! Fire!" several times to alert others. Each person should act as if there is intense smoke and crawl low to the floor while keeping one's head about one to two feet above the floor to breath cleanest air with least toxic fumes. Conduct drills at different times, both day and night. You might pull a surprise fire drill in the middle of the night.

Knowledge is Not Enough

I cannot emphasize enough the importance of escape planning and fire drills. Although I had talked with my family of the possibility of a fire and the need to get out quickly, we had not formally created a sensible plan, and practiced it. If we had, some mistakes we made during our escape may have been eliminated, allowing us to get out more quickly. The time delay nearly cost us our lives, as it does scores of people every year.

Benjamin Franklin who was a volunteer firefighter, said: "An ounce of protection is worth a pound of cure." His wisdom certainly applies when it comes to preparing your family and home for what you hope will never happen.

Practice Mentally

Smoke, panic, and toxic fumes cause disorientation. People have been found dead inside their own homes of many years because they thought they were heading for a safe exit, only to become disorientated and end up in laundry rooms, stairwells, or closets. Mental practice is good. Before the actual drill, have people mentally imagine what they will do to get out of their assigned location.

Make it Fun

Fire drills can be fun. In fact we learn faster when we're having fun than when we're anxious. So balance the fearful aspects with a little fun. Make it a game. A good exercise is to blindfold each person, one by one, walk them around a little to confuse them. Then time how long it takes to escape. While blindfolded have each household member experience the feel of the walls, flooring, and doors while crawling low and holding one's head in airspace just above the floor.

During the fire drill make sure that each person actually practices <u>each</u> step of escape, including crawling low to the floor.

Use a stopwatch to time how long it takes each person to carry out the steps of the drill. Always discuss what happened, how each person responded, how long it took and how they felt about it. You might have family members develop scenarios for each room and how one could get trapped in it. Then have everyone brainstorm what to do about it and role-play the best ideas to see how they would work.

Two or three run-throughs of the fire drill during the meeting is probably about right. Don't overload and stress people. Instead schedule another time when everyone is fresh to practice more. Include discussion of what to do if trapped by the fire.

Brief Home Workers

When hiring a cleaning person or babysitter, describe the household fire plan during the worker's orientation. Always remind babysitters of the fire escape plan each time they stay with your children. Don't be shy. The person works for you and safety of your children is paramount.

Make sure sitters, cleaning people and other home workers know the location of all the exits, where extinguishers are mounted, where fire ladders and disaster kits are stored and how to call 911. Stress that, with rare exceptions, they should not try to fight the fire. Stress to the sitter the importance of knowing where each child is at all times and to immediately act to get them out if a fire starts. Then, when the children are out of the building and at a safe distance, call 911 from a neighbor's house.

When the house has two or more stories, show home workers where the ladders are stored and how to unroll and attach them. When there is a baby or toddlers in the home, specifically instruct home workers to *carry* the baby out the exit or down the ladder. It is a good idea to include home workers and regular sitters in family fire drills. Of course, you will be expected to pay their wages for this training. It is money well spent.

Establish a Meeting Location

Establish a meeting area where everyone will gather after getting out of the house. This might be a particular place on the street in front of the house or at a neighbor's house, for example. Make sure the designated location is far enough away to be clear of heat, falling debris, smoke and toxic fumes. After everyone is accounted for, the family can share what each knows.

This is the time to account for pets and plan what to do next. With this method it can be quickly ascertained as to who has gotten out and who might be trapped inside. Make sure to designate a "Captain" and "Assistant Captain" to make decisions and give family members assignments, such as, "Go the neighbor and call 911."

Personal Papers

Protecting personal belongings requires special consideration. Valuable papers are likely to be detroyed by the heat, smoke, and water. The same holds true for computer data. If you store irreplaceable and difficult to reproduce data on floppy disks or tape you can lose it all in a fire. It doesn't take much heat, smoke, soot, or water to make the data worthless because it cannot be retrieved.

Protect Documents and Valuables

Discovering after a fire that your most important documents have burned is a major hassle. When our house burned, nearly all of the records, including the insurance policy, were destroyed by the fire and water from the fire. I knew I should have made copies of important documents, kept them in a separate location, such as a safe deposit box. But I failed to follow the recommendations I had made to thousands of clients I advised over the years. I had a computer, but backed up nothing to be kept offsite.

The insurance company needed receipts, photographs and video tapes to substantiate our loss. Video tapes show contents in detail, from small items to large pieces of furniture. But we had none to offer—only our word of what items we lost and their value and that wasn't good enough.

We still find ourselves looking for something only to realize that it was lost in the fire. These items were never put on the list because we didn't think of them when making the claim. You can't go back to the insurance company after the loss has been settled and say,. "Oh, by the way, we just remembered the fire consumed a precious piece of jewelry and valuable lamp". Once the claim is finally settled, it can not be reopened.

Losing irreplaceable mementos added to our trauma. Photos of family gatherings and relatives long gone could have been duplicated on a scanner. Scanners are available at copy centers for a small fee. Be fire safe—make duplicates and store them at a separate location.

Get a Fire Safe Container

Get a good fire resistant safe or a heavy strong box for storing valuable documents and small possessions. Safes come in various styles, including freestanding, wall safes, and floor safes placed in concrete slabs. A safe can be as small as a cigar box or big as a closet—or bigger.

Specialized safes that can keep the inside temperature during a fire low, while maintaining a safe level of humidity are available for protecting data on disks, floppies, and tapes.

The U.L. fire rating of safes is found on the label, which is usually affixed to the door. As a rule of thumb, a good home safe will be able to keep its interior under 212° F, the boiling point of water, while facing a 1700° F fire for a half-hour. To be effective in preserving your papers make sure you select a safe that is fire rated with at least a 1/2-hour rating, which means it can protect the contents from a fire up to 1700 degrees for 1/2 hour.

Make Copies

Make copies of precious items heirlooms and prized jewelry. Keep a set of documentary photos in the safe box so that you can substantiate what you own. Record the make and model numbers on a piece of paper and keep with your photos. This will assist your insurance company in establishing the value of the piece.

Store Copies Off-Site

Keep documents at a secure off-premises location, such as in a fire resistant safe at your attorney or stockbroker's office. If you have an apprisal on an expensive item, keep a duplicate of it in a separate off-site location.

Clutter like this is a double fire hazard. A candle, cigarette ash or short in the extention cord could ignite a fire. Once started, the clutter provides fuel to help flames spread rapidly.

 Disaster Kits

We should have had a disaster kit stocked with
clothing and other essentials to get us through the first
several days. Fortunately we had many friends and neighbors who helped us with clothing, blankets, food, even money.
Without their help, the fire would have been even more tramatic.

Recommended by Experts

The American Red Cross, FEMA, and nearly every disaster
preparedness organization recommends keeping a "disaster preparedness kit" suitable for your family's needs. In fact, it is smart to have
two kits, one kept in your home and second in your vehicle.

Commercially Made Kits

Disaster preparedness kits come in all shapes, sizes, and contents.
You can put one together yourself, or you can buy a ready-made one.
Having a professionally prepared kit is a good choice because they
contain a wide variety of items that you may not think of including.
Ready-made kits tend to be less expensive than purchasing the
individual items.

Location

A disaster kit must be easily accessible to be useful. That's why
major organizations suggest one in the home and one in the vehicle
because you might not be home when you need it. Keep home kit
items in a sturdy bag, box, or backpack that can be grabbed easily by
any family member on the way out of the house.

Don't store your kit high in a closet or cover it with other items
that would impede quick access. In our fire disaster we had just a
couple seconds to grab a kit as we exited the door—only we didn't
have one!

Personalize Your Disaster Kit

Recommended contents of disaster kits vary with family needs,
number of people it must sustain, medical conditions, and personal
factors, especially if there are children or elderly in your family. For
this reason—whether you design your own or purchase a kit—you
should personalize it to meet your family's specific requirements.

Essentials

First aid supplies are a must. Make sure to include a flashlight with extra batteries, so you can see in the dark, if the disaster occurs at night and the power goes out. Add at least a gallon of water for initial emergency use.

Include essential prescription medicines, which you or family members will need. Keep enough cash to purchase food, basic supplies, and clothing. Include snack bars and non-perishable foods. Blankets for each family member are important, along with supplies for babies and young children, such as diapers, formula, and basic care and first aid items specific for their needs. Don't forget keys for your car and safe, strongbox, or bank safe deposit box.

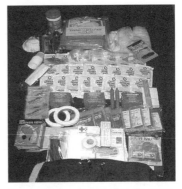

Start with a commercial disaster kit and add items, like glasses, keys and medicines, that you will need in an emergency.

Other Items

Other items to put into your disaster kit include thermal space blankets, waterproof ponchos, a battery operated radio with extra batteries, dust mask, can and bottle opener, knife, work gloves, disposable gloves, utensils, paper plates and cups, rope, tape, disposal bags, sheet plastic, antibacterial wipes, candles, waterproof matches, firesticks, collapsible water container, hand warmers, towels, scratchpad and pencil.

Lingering Trauma

Post Traumatic Stress Disorder, or PTSD, is the name for the emotional distress that can linger on after a traumatic event. The event could be a house fire, earthquake, hurricane, flood, tornado, a mugging or any other trauma that is sudden, overwhelming, and generally outside usual human experience.

We React Differently

Not everyone experiences a clinical definition of PTSD after a traumatic event. In fact less than 50% of the population does so. Nonetheless, nearly everyone endures some distress following a traumatic event for varying periods of time. Symptoms of PTSD may set in immediately or may be delayed for weeks, months, or even years. Symptoms must last for at least one month to meet the clinical definition. Symptoms lasting less than one month are classified as "acute stress disorder". Treatment and long-term expectations are similar regardless of the definition.

PTSD Symptoms

Shock and denial are typical responses to disasters and trauma. Denial is a normal protective reaction. Shock is a sudden and intense disturbance of emotional well-being, leaving the person feeling stunned or dazed. Denial involves refusing to acknowledge that the stressful event has occurred. Feeling numb and disconnected from life usually follows.

Symptoms of Acute Trauma

- Mood swings
- Sleep disruption
- Inability to concentrate
- Flashbacks and obessive recallections
- Anxiety and fear
- Nausea, headaches, and chest pain
- Withdrawal and irritability
- Fainting, dizziness, fever, paleness
- Feelings of guilt
- Crying spells, feelings of despair
- Lethargy
- Loss of appetite

Emotional Reactions

People who have lost their homes and/or loved ones in fires suffer long after the fire has been mopped up. They report having intense and sometimes unpredictable feelings, including depression and mood swings. They are more anxious, nervous and irritable than normal. They often become withdrawn and avoid social activities and get into frequent arguments with family members and co-workers.

Physical Reactions

Fire victims often experience nausea, headaches, and chest pain. Sometimes these symptoms are so severe that they require medical attention. Fainting, dizziness, fever, paleness, feelings of guilt over the event, agitation, changes in appetite, spontaneous crying, feelings of despair and hopelessness, and feeling low on energy are commonly experienced by people who have been in a major fire or lost their homes or loved ones to fire.

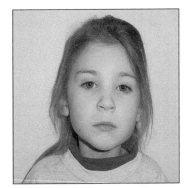

Children can be confused and frightened after a fire.

Lingering Trauma

Memories of the fire and its horrors effect daily life and interrupt sleep through nightmares. Fire victims report being unable to shake thoughts about the fire, what they "should" have done, and what they lost. They find it difficult to concentrate and startle easily. Vivid memories of the event and flashbacks often occur without warning leading to physical reactions such as sweating and rapid heartbeat. Sounds of sirens and the anniversary of the fire brings unpleasant thoughts, even fears that the event might repeat itself.

Factors Involved

Individual reactions to trauma and intensity vary greatly from person to person. Some people recover quickly, while others have lingering symptoms for years. Factors found to affect the length of time for recovery include the individual's ability to cope with difficult emotional situations. If the loss involved extensive property damage or loss of life, full recovery usually takes longer than that of a smaller fire, or one with no injuries.

Stressful events preceding the traumatic experience can effect recovery time. People who have been emotionally weakened by health problems, family difficulties, employment layoffs, money worries, and other draining problems tend to have more intense reactions to an additional trauma and usually take longer to recover. Introverts tend to react more strongly to traumatic events than extroverts.

Recovery

Recovery ranges from the symptoms fading over time, as they normally do, to the necessity for medical intervention with sedatives and psychotherapy. The form of treatment must be tailored to the individual. Personality, emotional state, and time since the fire influence recovery time. Getting away from the location where the fire occurred, plus several days of rest, possibly with use of relaxant drugs, are generally helpful.

Support of family and friends is invaluable. When an entire family or group of people have experienced the same event, the support system may be weakened, and in these cases support groups can be very effective. To locate support groups in your area, contact your local Red Cross, your family doctor or even a local hospital.

Getting Back to Normal

Speed of recovery is facilitated through reestablishment of routines such as eating meals at regular times and following an exercise program. Pursuing hobbies or other enjoyable activities, getting plenty of rest, and eating well-balance meals are helpful. Meditation and relaxation techniques are helpful, especially if sleep patterns have been interrupted. Taking a break from making important decisions is generally advised. It is also helpful for fire victims to learn about stress reactions and to understand that what they are experiencing is a normal adjustment process to loss.

Professional Help

Most people who have been through a traumatic fire experience demonstrate few symptoms and are able to fully recover using their own support systems. It is normal, however, for emotional distress to persist and negatively impact daily life. Those who have prolonged reactions that disrupt their daily functioning should seek help from their physician or other mental health providers. Psychologists can help in understanding what one experiences from trauma, what to expect, and can direct the fire victim toward recovery by finding constructive ways to deal with the emotional impact.

Children and Trauma

Children are especially vulnerable to the intense anxiety and fear associated with a fire. Careful attention needs to be paid to changes in mood, eating habits, sleep disturbances, tantrums, and other behavioral changes. Some children will regress and act younger than their age, exhibiting such behaviors as bed-wetting or thumb sucking. Parents and child care workers must determine if an experienced mental health professional should be consulted. Professional consultation is essential if a child exhibits extreme withdrawal, serious problems at school, continual and aggressive outbursts, unusually disturbed sleep and nightmares, or other intense emotional difficulties.

Alleviating Children's Fears

Structure is very comforting. Maintain regular eating, sleeping, and playtime schedules. Physical affection is soothing, especially to children. Allow them to cling, be near you, and to spend more time with you than you might do normally.

Children traumatized by fire need increased attention for several months after the experience. Tell them you understand their fears and anxiety. Encourage them to talk to you and others about their experience and be sure to listen with genuine concern. Let them know you are there to answer their questions, and do so in a way they can understand.

Children need special attention.

Younger children may be better able to demonstrate to you their fears in a nonverbal way, such as through drawing. Offering play experiences in which they can interact with you can be comforting to them and soften the anxiety.

🔥 Insurance

Homeowner policies are actually a "package" of coverages especially designed to meet the needs of homeowners. There are also special policies for condos owners, renters and owners of units in cooperatives.

The industry standard in homeowner policies has two parts. Section 1 covers the dwelling itself, other structures, personal contents and loss of use. Section 2 covers liability and medical coverage for injury and death. Standard homeowner policies do not cover damage from flood or earthquake.

Dwelling Coverage

The policy will have a specific stated amount of coverage for the main dwelling or home. This will be written in terms of "replacement cost" or "actual cash value". In most cases, you are better off with replacement cost and don't want the actual cash value coverage, which is depreciated. This means that a certain amount is deducted from the amount of the damage you sustained due to the age of the property. For example, if a kitchen, which is ten years old, is destroyed in a fire, your payment can be considerably less than it will cost to actually built a comparable kitchen.

The policy will state a value for your home.

Often the cost of replacement after fire damage is more than the amount for which the dwelling was insured. When the policy has replacement cost, the insurance company often pays more than the stated policy amount. However, all policies have limits on how much over the policy amount they will go in meeting replacement costs. These caps vary from state to state, company to company, and policy to policy. Whenever you take out a homeowner's policy that includes replacement cost make sure to ask about the specific terms and maximums.

Other Structures

Standard homeowner policies also include coverage for damage to other stuctures that are not attached to the dwelling. These include fences, pools, sheds, gazebos, children's play gyms and so forth. Generally, the amount of coverage is a percentage of the policy amount stated for the dwelling.

Personal Contents

Other structures include sheds.

Homeowner policies insure for damage to your personal property in the home for insured loss. Here again the coverage can be for actual cash value or for replacement costs. Personal property includes your clothes, furniture, nick nacks, personal computers, tools, bikes and other such items. Work equipment such as computers from your employer or copy machines and faxes used in a home business are usually not covered and require a separate policy, or special schedules. Fine art, expensive jewerly, furs, firearms, cash and other unique items are not covered, or only minimally so, under the policies standard provision. Coverage for these requires special forms or schedules which specify the item in detail and may require a professional appraisal supporting its value.

Loss of Use

Loss of use provision covers you for the costs you incur due to not being able to use your home. Generally this includes rent and utilities for temporary housing, possibility the cost of renting furniture. The amount of this coverage varies with the policy. In standard homeowner policy loss of use coverage is usually 20% of the stated, or insured value of the dwelling. In premier policies loss of use coverage can be as much as a full year of payments for alternative housing with no cap on the costs.

Schedules

Schedules are special attachments to the policy that either increase coverage for special items, like jewelry, coin collections, called floaters and riders. Other schedules limit your coverage, called exemptions. All homeowner policies exclude coverage for damage caused by flooding, for example.

Deductible

Deductible is that portion of the loss that the homeowner must pay. Standard policies have $250 deductible which means that you must pay the first $250 of the loss. You can raise the deductible to $500 or $1000, for example, which will reduce your premium.

Assume Some Risk

When you carry a higher deductible, such as $1000, you assume some of the risk. That is, small losses will be less than your deductible and you will not receive any payment from the insurance company. Often it is smart to carry a higher deductible because you will make fewer claims and run less of a chance that the insurance company will "non-renew" your policy, which often happens after you've made a few claims. Further, with a higher deductible you save a little on your premium, generally about $150 a year. This adds up to cover the small losses. In the industry this is called "managing your risk."

Discounts

Most companies offer discounts off the premium you pay for smoke detectors, central station alarm systems and other protective systems, as well as for being a non-smoker or retired.

Ask, Ask, Ask

Ask your agent questions to be sure that you understand your coverage..

Insurance policies are confusing and filled with industry buzz words. It is not always so clear to the lay person what they've bought. For example, suppose your policy says "replacement value". While it may seem obvious at first, there are many definitions of "replacement". What if your loss is greater than the amount for which you insured your home? One policy will cover the overage cost and the next won't. These are expensive distinctions. Never assume! Ask questions and then ask more questions. Make sure that you thoroughly understand what coverage you are buying.

Buying on the Internet

We've all heard the stories and seen the advertisements for cheap insurance available on the internet. And, in fact, numerous cheap policies are available and it is real insurance. The problem is that it is not so easy to know what coverage—specifically—you have purchased. As a broker friend of my said, "When buying online you can ask a lot of questions, but you won't get too many answers.

Advertisements for online insurance sales usually stress that they have no agents—you interface directly with the company—and this means lower premiums. But the flip side of this is that you have no person to call and no one is assigned to you—waiting to help you.

Agents vs Brokers

An insurance broker holds a license to sell insurance. In most cases agents work for only one insurance company. The agent can answer more questions, but only about the policies issued by that one company. Such agents are called, "captured agents." Still, such an agent is beholden to you and responsible for servicing your needs relative to your policy. Often, you can have the same agent for years, even decades and develop a close, trusting relationship.

A broker can also be licensed to work as an agent, i.e., writing policies. The difference is that a broker/agent usually works for several insurance companys. This means that he or she can shop around to get you better coverage for your particular needs rather than always selling you one company's products.

In our case, we purchased insurance through a major insurance company that did not assign agents to clients. The agent who wrote our policy did service our account. Consequently, when I called in with the cancellation problem I could not ask for a particular agent, instead any agent on duty that day was expected to take care of our problem. We didn't have a one-on-one relationship with anyone. No one person was accountable to us—or even knew who I was when I called. I was just a policy number and voice on the phone. Had we been insured by a company that assigned agents (which costs more, as you would expect) I could have called my agent directly—possibly even at home and would have had our uninsured status quickly corrected.

Fail-Safe

Insurance companies are required to give policyholders sufficient notices—the length of which varies from state to state—that they intend to cancel or not renew your policy. Typically it is 30 days. If you fail to pay your premium, your policy will be "cancelled". Cancellations have a shorter notice period. Sometimes the insurance company elects to not renew your policy, which is called "non-renewal.". They may not renew your policy because there is something about the property that that's a problem, such as being in run-down condition. Other times, the insurance company has stopped offering the type of policy you have.

When you have an assigned agent, he or she receives duplicate notices. If you haven't paid, your agent will usually call to remind you. In some cases, if you have several policies with the same agent, he or she will actually pay your premium for you, such as when you are on vacation, for example. When an agent receives a notice of non-renewal of your policy, your agent will usually get right to work on finding alternative coverage. Again, if you have several policies with the agent and your non-renewal is due to a defect in the property, he or she can sometimes intervene and get the non-renewal decision reversed. For example, a friend of mine, Sharon who has several rentals all handled by the same agent. When she got a non-renewal for debris being in the yard (her student tenants were moving out), the agent drove about 35 miles to the rental, took photos showing that it had been cleaned up and sent them to the company which reversed its decision to non-renew.

Cheaper is Not Better

When you purchase an insurance policy online without an agent, you are, in effect, acting as your own agent. You do all of this yourself. It is a little cheaper. We didn't have an assigned agent. So when we didn't get the non-renewal notice saying that they discontinued our policy, we had no fail-safe. As luck would have it, our home burned down just two nights after the policy expired. Our loses far out weighed the small savings on the discounted policy.

Lender Policies

If you have a bank loan or a private lender, they will require that you have sufficient insurance to cover their risk—the amount you owe. The lender requires that they be listed on your policy. However, this doesn't happen automatically. You must instruct your insurance company to list your mortgagee as an "additionally insured" on your policy.

Should your policy be cancelled or not renewed, the insurance company will send a notice to your lender—provided that they are listed on the policy. If your policy does, in fact, terminate without your having secured new coverage, your lender will automatically insure the property. The catch is that they insure it for the amount of *their risk only*—which is the principle balance due on your mortage. If your property has appreciated since buying it, if you made a big down payment or you've made a lot of extra principle payments, you can be in a situation of being seriously under insured. If your mortgage is for fifty thousand, for example, but your property is worth five hundred thousand, the bank will insure it for only fifty thousand.

Another, downside is that your lender insures only the dwelling and other structures, not the contents or your loss of use. So, as happened to us, we lost everything, even our clothes. We had no coverage. The lender's insurance paid to rebuild the house but that was all. Finally, lender insurance is very expensive, often triple what you may have been paying—or more!

Be Pro-Active

If you elect to go without an agent, don't depend on the insurance company to get notices of renewal to you. There are too many ways of not receiving timely notices. In many states insurance companies are not required to send renewal notices by registered mail or to give you a courtesy phone call. Mark the expiration dates on your calendar. When your policy is near lapsing, use a delivery method that requires a signature, or personally deliver payment it to your insurer, and get a written receipt.

Should you discover, as we did, that your policy has expired, you can go on line and procure a new policy. Better to have double coverage, than none at all, as what happened to us. You can always cancel the online policy in a few days when you have something better in place. You'll probably get some refund of your premium. The cost is minimal compared to the risk.

Documentation

To determine what you own, make a list of all your household belongings. Whenever you can, write down the prices and dates of purchase. Take videotape or photographs of everything, if possible, and of at least your more valued belongings. Keep the written and photographic records in a safe place, outside your home such as in a safe deposit box or other secure location. A thorough and up-to-date inventory list can save a significant amount of money in the event that a fire does strike.

Take an Inventory

A good inventory is extremely important in negotiating a settlement with the insurance company. They will want evidence to back up your claim.

To make a good inventory record of your belongings walk through the house recording with a video camera or still camera. Describe all the furniture and valuables as you film the items. When using a still camera, photograph all furniture and objects within each room, within cabinets and drawers. Then photograph general panoramic shots of each room.

Take good photographs and write down descriptions of every high value item, especially those that would have individual policy limits and must be included on a special schedule.

Another helpful hint is to keep sales receipts from purchases of household possessions. Keep cancelled checks and credit card receipts as additional proof of your ownership of the items and its cost. Making a complete inventory before purchasing or renewing a policy can help determine just what and how much coverage you need to purchase.

Insurance Adjuster

The insurance adjuster will visit the location of the loss within hours of your disaster. Be ready to meet with the adjuster. Locate your inventory, insurance policy, and collect your thoughts as to what was destroyed and damaged. The adjuster will take photographs and make a written list of damaged and destroyed items. They will need your help in identification. This identification and inventory process of the insurance company is where your good documentation really pays off.

Of course the adjuster works for the insurance company and not for you. Naturally, the adjuster's objective is to keep the claim as low as possible. This is where having an invenotry of what was in the house with photos pays off. These documents help you to persuade the adjuster of the value of your loss and help the adjuster justify the claim, especially if it is large, to the insurance company. Often you will disagree with the adjuster about the value of certain items or if certain things are covered. Here is where is it really helps to have an agent who can go to bat for you. If your agent is also a broker, who represents many companys, that's even better because he or she will have a larger perspective and won't be so worried about the reaction of one insurance company's policies—as an agent who represents only one company might be.

Your inventory will assist the adjuster in determining the amount of your loss.

🔥 Away From Homes

Thousands die and many more are injured annually in burning hotels and motels. Just as there are certain precautions you can take at home, awareness and precautions are effective in lowering the chances of being injured or dying in a fire when staying away from home.

Hotels & Motels

A survey of vacationers conducted by the NFPA revealed the biggest concern was fire safety at lodging facilities. There are literally thousands of lodging facilities scattered across the U.S. with minimal fire protection. Even some of the most expensive and finest hotels can be are lax in their fire procedures. Hotels are inherently a fire problem because they are populated by all types of people, some who smoke and some who do not, some careful and others not so careful. When asleep we are slower to detect smoke. Decision making abilities are reduced when first awakened. When staying in a hotel or motel—even when at a friend's home—you may be at risk.

Ask About Safety

All lodging facilities in the U.S. and Canada are required by law to have operational smoke detectors in the rooms and all public areas. Although that is the law, I have personally seen many who are in violation. When booking ask if the rooms have smoke detectors and if they are tied into a central monitoring system that operates 24/7. A central detection system is no good if there is no one there to monitor it. Inquire about their smoking policy, sprinklers and emergency lighting in the halls?. Note: Bring a good flashlight anyway—just in case. Find out if there is a restaurant or kitchen in which cooking is performed. Restaurants and kitchens are often the point of origin for commercial fires. You might request that you are booked into a room away from such a potential hazard.

Be fire safe when on vacation.

Mini Fire Drill

After you get your luggage into your room, locate the smoke detectors and test them by pressing the "test" button. If it doesn't operate properly call "Housekeeping" and request a replacement or call the "Desk" and ask to be moved to another room.

Locate the fire extinguisher nearest to your room, review the operating instructions and check its inspection tags. If it is expired, call "Housekeeping" and request that they replace it with a newly inspected extinguisher. Don't be shy. Hotels are not cheap and this is your life.

Evaculation Plan

An evacuation plan should be posted inside your room, probably on the door. If there is no fire evacuation plan posted in your room, request one and study it. Then go out into the hall and follow the egress route specified in the plan. As you do so, count the number of doors between your room and the exit to the outside. This is important, because it is easy to get disoriented during the crisis of a fire, with the smoke, confusion and being in a strange place. This is a kind of fire drill that will give you a better chance of getting out

Find the nearest fire alarm and study the instructions.

safely if there is a fire. Remember, never use elevators to escape a fire.

Locate the fire alarm nearest to your room and read the operating instructions posted on it. If you must activate a fire alarm in dense smoke you will be better prepared by having done this first. It takes only a few minutes.

Keep your room key in your pocket all the times until you go to bed, then put it on the nightstand where you can grab it quickly. You might not be able to find your clothes or be able to put them on in an emergency. You may need to retreat back to your room if the hallways leading to exits are filled with smoke or fire. Many people have survived hotel and motel fires by staying in their rooms until rescued.

Some experts suggest asking for rooms on the seventh floor or lower in the front, because most fire departments have ladders that will reach up to seven floors. You'll be seen yelling from the front of the building, whereas when your room is on one of the light wells, no one will see you. If the windows open, test that they are working properly. Look out the window to determine where you might be able to jump or climb onto a ledge if you had to.

Remember:

Be fire safe!

Dr. Steven Shepard

Steven C. Shepard Ph.D. has an extensive background in residential and commercial property loss control, disaster counseling, life safety, real estate design and development, and psychology.

For 17 years he owned and operated a highly successful loss control company, whose clients were among the largest U.S. insurance companies, including Allstate, Fireman's Fund, Farmers, Ohio Casualty, Lumberman's Mutual, Hartford, Golden Eagle, American States, and others. Focusing on fire, wind, water, and earth movement, he advised his customers of methods to limit or eliminate property damage, injury or loss of life. He leads insurance seminars, writes loss control articles, and appears regularly on radio and television.

Steven Shepard and family narrowly escaped with their lives when a fire ravaged their family home. Dr. Shepard lives with his wife and daughter in rural Montana, where he continues his research, writing, Life Protectors, which supplies disaster preparedness products, along with operating a full time ranch and farm.

Dr. Shepard can be contacted through his website: www.LifeProtectors.com. Please visit.

Quantity Discounts

Be Fire Safe helps prevent fires and saves lives. It makes a wonderful gift and fund raiser give-away. Order three or more copies and receive a generous discount. Ronin Publishing is happy to prepare a special premium edition in quantities over 3000 for your company or association.

Discount & Shipping Schedule*

3 to 5 copies	15% discount from retail + $5 shipping
6 to 15 copies	25% discount from retail + $7 shipping
16 to 25 copies	35% discount from retail + $9 shipping
26 to 35 copies	40% discount from retail + $11 shipping
36 to 50 copies	45% disocunt from retail + $12 shipping
51 to 100 copies	50% discount from retail + $15 shipping
Over 100 copies	call for large quantity discounts

*Terms and prices subject to change without notice

ORDER FORM

_____ Quantity of books ordered

_____ x $10.95 or current retail price

_____ Subtotal

_____ x discount - see schedule above

_____ Subtotal

_____ x 8.25% sales tax (Orders shipping to Calif address)

_____ + Ship fee (See schedule - USA* only)

_____ = Total amount due.

___ Check enclosed   Charge my ___ Visa __MC

Exp date __/__ Card # ___/___/___/___

Name _____

Address _____Apt #_____

City _____ State ___ Zip _____

Telephone _____ Email _____

Mail Order Form and payment to RONIN PUBLISHING, PO Box 522, Berkeley, CA 94701

For more information or to place an order by phone, call 510/420-3669 or email order@roninpub.com

*International orders shipped airmail or global priority and calculated at current rate.